SURVIVE
SNOW COUNTRY

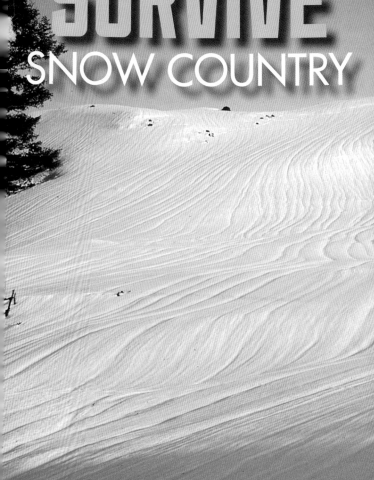

SURVIVE

SNOW COUNTRY

JEFF HENRY

FALCON®

Guilford, Connecticut

To my dad, Jack Henry, and to all the others who have suffered from Alzheimer's disease.

FALCON®

An imprint of Globe Pequot
Falcon and FalconGuides are registered trademarks and Make Adventure Your Story is a trademark of Rowman & Littlefield.

Distributed by NATIONAL BOOK NETWORK

Copyright © 2017 by Rowman & Littlefield

All rights reserved. No part of this book may be reproduced in any form or by any electronic or mechanical means, including information storage and retrieval systems, without written permission from the publisher, except by a reviewer who may quote passages in a review.

Photos by Jeff Henry unless otherwise credited

British Library Cataloguing-in-Publication Information available

Library of Congress Cataloging in Publication Data available

ISBN 978-1-4930-2385-1 (paperback)
ISBN 978-1-4930-2386-8 (e-book)

∞™ The paper used in this publication meets the minimum requirements of American National Standard for Information Sciences—Permanence of Paper for Printed Library Materials, ANSI/NISO Z39.48-1992.

CONTENTS

ACKNOWLEDGMENTS

Several people provided advice, information, or anecdotes for this book. For such contributions I would like to thank Jason Fatourous, Ron Wilkes, Shane Roos, Michael Keator, Rebekah Houck, Crystal Cassidy, Virgia Bryan, Jenny Wolfe, Scott Hamilton, Louise Mercier, and Joe Bueter.

I also would like to thank the following people for their contributions of photographs or other illustrations: Larry Lahren of Anthro Research in Livingston, Montana; Jerry Brekke, historical consultant in Livingston, Montana; Eric Knoff of the Gallatin National Forest Avalanche Center in Bozeman, Montana; Peter Lewis of the Stonehearth Open Learning Opportunities (SOLO) School in Conway, New Hampshire; Mariah Gale Henry for compiling the wind-chill chart; Lisa Culpepper of Culpepper Photography in Gardiner, Montana; and Jim Halfpenny of A Naturalist's World in Gardiner, Montana.

INTRODUCTION

If you have picked up this book and are reading these words, you're probably like me in the sense that you enjoy winter and snow and the sports that go with them. Indeed, it's hard for me to fathom that there is anyone who *doesn't* like snow and cold weather.

Winter scenes are breathtakingly beautiful, and there is such a sense of wonder and romance in the snow itself. As for winter sports, who could not like touring through winter wonderlands in a car or on a snowmobile, to say nothing of lovely snowshoe treks through winter-whitened woods, or schussing downhill on skis? For me, and for many of my friends, activities like those are about as good as it gets.

But, of course, there is a flip side to wintry weather and snowy environments. Weather can change quickly. Snowmobiles can break down and cars can get stuck in the snow, while snowshoers and cross-country skiers can wind up lost or injured in the backcountry.

The purpose of this book is to help you avoid winter-related problems in the first place. Second, the book contains information that hopefully will help you deal with survival problems that can and often do occur in wintry situations.

To write the book, I have drawn on a lifetime of working and playing in the snow. As much as possible I have arranged my life to spend a maximum amount of time outdoors in the winter, working jobs like wildlife researcher, park ranger, freelance photographer specializing in winter subjects, and more. My favorite avocation for almost forty years has been sawing snow from tourist buildings in Yellowstone National Park to prevent them from collapsing under winter's weight. While I have spent most of my time in the wintry outdoors alone, I have never suffered a significant injury or otherwise fallen into any sort of serious predicament. As an old-timer I once knew used to say, the difference between livin' and dyin' is knowin', and hopefully this book will help you learn some of what is necessary to get by in the snowy world of winter.

HIKING IN SNOW COUNTRY

It may seem paradoxical, but there are probably more hikers who become lost or injured in the snow than there are people who engage in classic winter sports like snowmobiling, cross-country skiing, or snowshoeing. That's simply because there are more hikers than there are pure winter recreationists, and it's also true that hikers are probably less likely to be prepared for wintry conditions. Hunters can be grouped with hikers, and they are notorious for finding themselves in snowy predicaments.

Hunters Chris and Jill Gastrock head off into the snowy backcountry.

Typically, most hikers start out in conditions of little or no snow. They often find themselves in trouble when they have hiked too far, especially after they've hiked far enough to get into higher and snowier mountains, or if they are still out when the weather changes and it begins to snow. No matter how you arrive in a snow-related emergency, your comfort and perhaps even survival depend on the interrelated basic considerations of staying dry, staying warm, and staying hydrated and well fed.

Because hikers don't usually hike in extremely wintry conditions, it's unlikely the snow will be either deep enough or consolidated enough to build emergency snow shelters like igloos or snow trenches. Given the likelihood that a lost day hiker won't have a tent or other portable refuge either, one of the best options for emergency shelter is a wickiup. Simply tie three relatively straight saplings together at the top, spread the poles out at the bottom, and then continue to add more poles to the basic tripod until the enclosure is complete (see photo). If a tarp is available, it can be draped over the outside of the structure as a shield from wind and water. If no tarp is on hand, progressively smaller-diameter poles can be added to the outside of the cone to seal off the enclosure, and foliated branches on the outside of the frame can make it even more air- and watertight. Leave a small gap in the perimeter to serve as a doorway—a small tarp, an extra garment, or a densely foliated shrub or branch can be used as a door flap after you've gone inside.

The size of the wickiup is determined, of course, by the length of the poles used to construct it. A small fire inside the wickiup will heat the whole structure. If possible, green poles and foliage make the best wickiup, as they are less likely to ignite from radiant heat or wayward sparks from the fire. The beauty of a wickiup's conelike shape is that much of a fire's heat will stay down low in the structure, where it will warm the occupants. Another tip: It's best if the inner poles of the structure are de-limbed and smooth. That way any seeping meltwater will tend to adhere to the poles and run down them to the ground rather than drip into the wickiup's interior.

An original American Indian wickiup in the snow, probably built no later than about 1880, northern Rocky Mountains

In addition to wickiups, there are other types of emergency shelters that can be built in the absence of a tent or other prefab unit, and built from naturally occurring materials. A simple lean-to will work as a rain and snow shelter and as a partial wind block, and of course a fire can be built on the open side of the structure. A low, wedge-shaped enclosure (see photo above) can be built out of a combination of poles and sticks, with the low end of the wedge designed to shelter the feet and ankles and the larger, open end of the structure designed as an entrance and to cover the head and upper end of the body. The interior of the wedge can be lined with dry leaves or grass if such dry material is available. Green conifer boughs can be used inside the wedge for bedding as well. Of course, it makes sense to keep all building and bedding materials as dry as possible by first scraping the site clean and then by shaking off as much snow from the materials as possible.

I remember constructing a wedgelike shelter in 1983 while hunting elk in the mountains of southern Montana. That occasion was not an emergency—I just wanted to spend a night out in remote country, which had taken me a full day of hiking to access, and my little structure afforded me a snug and warm place to spend the night in a lovely setting of snow-covered conifers and mountains. Camping out made it possible for me to see the sun rise over the beautiful scene the next morning.

In some respects hunters have an advantage over other hikers in that they tend to carry more items that can be useful in an emergency situation. Knives, saws, and rope or other twine are included in this list. On the other hand, in their pursuit of quarry and in their desire to get away from competition, hunters are sometimes more likely to travel farther into the backcountry and to pay less attention to time constraints, and therefore are more likely to find themselves in a fix when the weather changes or daylight begins to wane.

EMERGENCY FIRE BUILDING

It's even more critical to have fire-making materials with you. I always stress that it's important to carry at least two different ways to build a fire. I absolutely always carry, as a minimum, a cigarette lighter as well as matches. Waterproof matches are preferable, and whether waterproof or not I always carry them in a plastic bag—and I almost always carry at least two cigarette lighters. If I am going out for an extended period of time, or often just as a matter of course, I also carry a magnesium fire striker.

It's best to have several different ways to start a fire because in my experience no method is infallible. Matches can get wet, of course, and even waterproof matches can lose their effectiveness by having their striking heads abraded away by rubbing inside your pack. And I have noticed that the lighter fluid in cigarette lighters becomes less likely to vaporize and ignite as temperatures get colder. I have also seen the striking wheel on the head of a lighter break off after it gets crushed or pinched inside a pack or a pants pocket. The magnesium fire striker seems less prone to failure, but using one effectively takes some practice and also requires the use of a knife. Starting a fire by any method becomes more difficult as temperatures fall—not just because your hands and fingers become less dexterous but also because fuel of all types becomes more difficult to ignite as things get colder.

No matter the method, it is important to meticulously assemble your tinder and kindling, and to carefully prepare your fire site, before you begin your efforts to start a fire. I can't emphasize this point enough—so often people in urgent need of a fire will cut corners and not take sufficient time to have everything organized beforehand. It is common, for example, to see someone kindle a little blaze and then leave it to go collect larger pieces of kindling.

Hunters in the backcountry scanning a fog-filled valley below

By the time the person returns with the larger twigs, the nascent fire may have gone out for want of fuel—far better to have your matches or lighter, your tinder and kindling, and some larger fuel all assembled before you even begin trying to strike a spark. Shelter from the wind and proximity to accessible fuel are also important considerations.

It's also important, or at least very helpful, to carry some sort of tinder and/or fire accelerant with you for emergencies. Dryer lint works really well, as do cotton balls impregnated with petroleum jelly. Wax paper is another good option, as it will burn even when wet. I carry it in some sort of unbreakable container with a threaded lid that can be tightly screwed shut. But to reiterate what is perhaps the most important point: When it comes to building an emergency fire, always remember the old adage that it's never wise to rush that which has to be done quickly.

Whether out hunting or hiking for some other outdoor interest, it is far better to not get lost or injured or caught outside at the onset of a winter storm in the first place. Carry a compass and appropriate maps, and know how to use them. Knowing the weather forecast is also important, as is the ability to read the weather yourself once you are out in the backcountry. Carrying survival gear like fire-starting materials and extra clothing are paramount, and knowledge of first aid and carrying first-aid supplies are important as well. A headlamp, some twine (like parachute cord), and a multipurpose knife are just about indispensable too. High-energy snacks and adequate clean water are musts. For winter outings it's preferable to carry metal water bottles rather than plastic ones—empty metal containers can be filled with snow and placed near a fire so the snow will melt into liquid water. Consuming warm water is a great way to incorporate more warmth into your metabolic equation.

CROSS-COUNTRY SKIING

Graceful, fluid, healthful, and more—cross-country skiing is a beautiful way to get around when the snow is deep. There is good reason why this mode of winter transportation evolved thousands of years ago and has persisted ever since. For most purposes and in almost all snow conditions, skiing is far more efficient than snowshoeing.

One of the many advantages of cross-country (aka Nordic) skiing is that the basics can be learned rather quickly. After just a half day or so of instruction, the average person is able to at least shuffle around on top of deep snow that otherwise would be impossible to negotiate. Enthusiasts can then continue to improve on cross-country skiing techniques and knowledge for the rest of their lives.

A well-clothed and well-equipped cross-country skier in the Gallatin Mountain Range, southern Montana

In addition to simply being a way to move across snow that is too deep for walking, cross-country skiing has evolved into a sport that includes track skiing on groomed trails. Since it is not likely that a person engaged in track skiing will encounter a survival situation, we are not as concerned about those incarnations of cross-country skiing here. Tour skiing is what leads people into the backcountry, and it is the sort of skiing that most interests us.

SOME CROSS-COUNTRY SKI BASICS

Skis for touring are sized according to a person's height and weight, and to a lesser extent by the snow conditions where the person intends to travel. As a general rule, touring skis should reach to a person's wrist when the arm is stretched above the head. Cross-country ski poles should reach to a person's armpits.

Skis come in two general types—waxable and waxless. Color-coded and temperature-coordinated waxes are used on the former type to somewhat miraculously provide traction as a skier kicks forward while simultaneously allowing for glide as the skier strides ahead or cruises downhill. Waxless skis, on the other hand, feature various sorts of patterns on their undersides that in a basic sense are collections of inclined planes, with the slanted surface of each little plane angling ahead and the right-angle edge of each plane facing toward the rear of the ski. The little inclines allow for forward glide while resisting backward motion, as when a skier moves forward or skis uphill.

The undersides of both types of skis are coated from end to end with a base wax, which not only allows for smoother passage over the snow but also helps prevent the buildup of ice and caked snow. The base wax is different from the color-coded wax used on waxable skis, which is known as kicker wax and is applied to only a fairly short segment of the ski under the skier's foot. As a general rule, waxable skis are capable of a higher level of performance provided they are waxed correctly for existing snow and temperature conditions. Waxless skis are generally better during times of rapidly changing conditions, such as you might encounter on a late winter/early spring ski.

It's important to pay special attention to clothing while engaged in cross-country skiing. It's necessary to have clothing that can be arranged to allow for the dissipation of body heat (and especially for dissipating bodily moisture) for times when you're skiing hard and/or the air temperatures and sunshine are warm. On the other hand, you have to be able to rearrange the same clothing or put on additional clothing to stay warm when temperatures fall and you're no longer putting out enough energy to keep yourself warm.

Wanda Sue Williams adjusts her clothing layers while on a cross-country ski trip in the Absaroka Mountains, southern Montana.

Heavy garments like bulky parkas don't lend themselves well to cross-country skiing—they not only tend to impede a skier's motions but also can quickly lead to overheating. Instead, layering your clothing is key, and foundationally that starts with polypropylene or some sort of synthetic underwear that wicks moisture away from the skin. The best option for the next layer is probably some sort of fleece for both the legs and the upper body. On top of the fleece it's best to have water- and windproof pants and jacket. Depending on weather and how far you intend to ski, extra clothing, such as additional fleece garments, can be carried in a pack. A cap or a full ski mask is also a must, at least to be carried in a pack and donned as necessary.

Particular attention should be paid to the hands while skiing. If you lose function of your fingers, you can really find yourself in dire straits because you won't be able to do much to help yourself. I like fleece gloves, and I supplement them with wool or fleece mittens that I carry in my pack for whenever I might need them. Gloves are better for controlling ski poles, but mittens are obviously better when the weather is colder. And when it's really cold, you can put your mittens on over your gloves to double up the insulation.

It's also a good idea to carry chemical hand warmers to use when the weather turns really cold, or when your hands are cold and need some supplemental heat to return to functionality.

Chemical heat packs are an indispensable ace in the hole for any sort of winter outing. They are light to carry and easy to use, and provide a quick heat subsidy to the hands. The boost of warmth can range from being

Backcountry ski group in Hayden Valley, Yellowstone National Park

somewhat helpful, as in easing the discomfort of a mild chill, to being critically important by restoring dexterity to fingers that have lost their function and reached the point where they cannot do what has to be done to save your own life (or the lives of your companions).

Since your feet are literally in the snow when you're skiing, you have to pay special attention to them as well. If you are prone to having cold feet, it might work best to layer some sort of thin undersock, possibly one made out of polypropylene, and then wool socks, but there are so many different fabrics on the market today that it's mostly a matter of each person making up his or her own mind as to what works best on an individual basis. Considerations like insulation, cushioning, protection from blistering, and more must be taken into account and balanced. Chemical heat packs sized and configured specifically for the feet can also be a good idea for those inclined to having cold feet.

I am a firm believer in gaiters to wear over the ankle. There is a wide variety to choose from, so once again it is up to the individual to pick the ones that work the best according to personal needs and expected conditions.

Physical fitness is a crucial component of being prepared for outdoor activities. This only makes sense—a tired skier is more likely to have an accident and suffer an injury, or to simply tire out and not be able to complete the planned trip. Suffering from either an injury or exhaustion, a skier can be in dire straits indeed if he or she is physically unable to respond to the situation and take appropriate survival measures. A related consideration is to know your own abilities and limitations, and to not ski farther away from your starting point than your level of fitness will allow (bearing in mind the time and energy required for the return trip as well). It's also important to know your skill level as a skier, and to not try to ski something that is beyond your abilities, which might result in an injury.

Important too is the ability to read terrain and snow. There are all sorts of different types of snow—fresh snow, old snow, loose snow, drifted snow, and so on, almost without end, and each type means something different for a skier. It is worthwhile, for example, to know when a swale in the snow indicates a watercourse flowing underneath, and to know whether the sagging snow bridge over the stream is strong enough to hold a passing skier. And it goes without saying that you should be able to read terrain and snow to the point where you can recognize sites with potential avalanche danger. (See the Avalanches chapter.)

The ability to read snow, as in deciding where to cross the stream in this photograph, is an important backcountry skill.

For cross-country skiing survival gear, I recommend carrying parachute cord, an avalanche shovel and avalanche beacon, fire-starting materials, a waterproof tarp, a map and compass (at least when venturing into unfamiliar country), and some sort of waterproof pad to keep you dry and insulated from the snow while sitting or lying down. As a personal choice you may also elect to carry a cell phone, a personal locator device, or some other sort of GPS equipment, although I believe their usefulness is frequently limited by topography and weather, and personally I do not like their presence intruding on my experience in the backcountry.

For emergency repairs of ski equipment itself, I recommend carrying a replacement ski tip. A friend of mine named Louise Mercier once broke a ski tip while on a demanding ski trip near the Old Faithful area in Yellowstone National Park. Because Louise hadn't carried a replacement tip on the trip, she had to face a long trudge through deep snow to get back to where she started. Fortunately, she was young and strong, and snow conditions were such that she was able to manage the trip out (with help from her companion and by postholing for many miles), although it took a great deal of time and effort to do so.

I further recommend carrying a generous amount of duct tape, which is most conveniently carried by wrapping a length of the tape around the shaft of each of your ski poles. A multipurpose knife with screwdriver options can be very useful, for when the screws in your ski binding pull loose.

The items mentioned here are a minimum, and since cross-country skiing and snowshoeing are in many ways similar, a more comprehensive list is included as a sidebar in the chapter on snowshoeing.

Perhaps most important of all is to cultivate a sense of creativity, to be flexible and adaptive to conditions and developments. In the scenario of a binding pulling loose from a ski, I have more than once re-secured things by breaking off a small twig and inserting it into the screw socket to shim it tighter before I replaced the loosened screw. I have also taken the time to melt a little snow with my hands and fingers, and use the resultant water to soak the twig before inserting it into the screw hole. That way the twig will first swell with the water, and then freeze in place in its socket to better hold the reinserted screw.

Most sources would recommend not skiing alone. Most of the same sources would say that it's important to have at least two people on a ski outing, and ideally at least three. There is merit to those recommendations—a skier alone who suffers a disabling injury in the snow is indeed in serious trouble. If the injured skier has a companion, the second person can take survival measures for the injured party. With three people in a party, one can stay with the injured skier while the other goes for help.

Most sources would also recommend leaving a travel itinerary with a responsible party before embarking on a ski tour. There is merit to that suggestion too. But here's what I think: I am not averse to skiing with other people—I have many friends, and skiing is one way I like to spend time with them. But I also like to ski alone, much as I like to hike alone in the summer, and I have done both all my life. There is an element of risk. But the way I figure it, if you can't be alone in this world when you go on a cross-country ski trip through wintry surroundings, where and when can you be alone? And to me, that's a big part of the reason to go skiing or on any other backcountry outing in the first place, to get away from the rush and hurry, the noise and confusion,

Crossing a backcountry stream on a fallen log

Another way to cross a stream

and the general stress of modern-day life, and to have time to contemplate your surroundings and reflect on how you as an individual fit into it all. Learn and practice the survival techniques with others on numerous trips, then make up your own mind before you cross-country ski by yourself.

As far as leaving an itinerary and anticipated return time/day with someone before you go—well, it doesn't hurt to do so, but realistically you will still have to be able to take care of yourself for an extended time. Even in the best-case scenario, it could be days before someone mounts a search adequate to find you.

SNOWSHOEING

PURPOSES OF SNOWSHOES

Snowshoes are not as fast, and for the most part not as fun, as skis, but I do believe 'shoes have their uses. In some snow conditions, especially early in the winter before the season's first snows have had time to set up, snowshoes' superior flotation allows you to stay on top of the snow, whereas skis sometimes flounder. Snowshoes allow for more careful movement over terrain, and therefore were historically more suited for hunters and trappers who wanted to move stealthily in their search for quarry.

The author's snowshoe trail leads to the top of a ridge to photograph a beautiful winter sunrise.

Snowshoes are inherently more stable than skis, and for that reason are the choice for many in pursuits like wildlife observation and photography. Snowshoes have frequently been my preferred option for photographic outings—their stable platform is usually better for manipulating cameras, changing lenses, and the like. And this is from someone who really, really likes to cross-country ski.

Aesthetically, snowshoes made from artificial materials are nowhere near as pleasing to me as the wood and rawhide models, and in my experience and observation, snow tends to pile up on the surface of models with a continuous deck under the foot. The snowshoer then has to lift the added weight of the piled-up snow off the ground with each stride. Snowshoes with cross lacing, on the other hand, tend to shed snow down through the openings in the laces each time the foot is picked up, at least in most snow conditions. A further benefit of snowshoes with wooden frames and natural lacings is that they tend to be quieter than models made with metal and plastic. Again, in my mind that is more aesthetic and also more practical for anyone

Snowshoes are often the choice of people involved with wildlife, like wolf researcher Matt Becker in Wyoming.

who desires subtlety for the sake of an activity like bird watching or wildlife photography.

Because snowshoers travel at slower speeds than cross-country skiers, and because you are not as likely to lose your balance on 'shoes, snowshoers are less likely to suffer disabling injuries. Knee injuries are not uncommon, however, and snowshoers are as apt to become lost or disoriented as are skiers or hikers. They are also subject to most of the other risks common to all winter enthusiasts, such as hypothermia, avalanches, and the like.

Snowshoes can be a good way to get into the backcountry and see things like this bison herd in Yellowstone National Park.

TYPES OF SNOWSHOES

Snowshoes come in a wide array of shapes and sizes. Generally, models with rounded tails are better for traveling up and down sloping terrain such as that found in the Rocky Mountains. Models with tapered tails are more suited to traveling through thick brush in more level country, like much of Minnesota, for instance. Long and tapered tails allow brush to slip off the back of the snowshoe instead of tangling on the foot or the snowshoe itself as a snowshoer strides forward. Various types of cleats can be affixed to the bottom of snowshoes for traction on ice or crusty snow.

It is easier for a novice to achieve a reasonable level of proficiency with snowshoes than with cross-country skis, and that is one reason for the increasing popularity of snowshoes in recent years.

SIZING SNOWSHOES

Snowshoes are sized according to the size and weight of the prospective snowshoer, and also according to expected snow conditions.

Heavier people need larger snowshoes, of course. As a general rule, those weighing in the 100- to 140-pound range can get by with snowshoes as short as 20 to 22 inches. People weighing 200 pounds or more should select 'shoes in the 36- to 48-inch range (or sometimes longer). If you have plans to carry a backpack or other gear, the weight of those items must be taken into account too, as do snow conditions. Light, fluffy snow requires more "flotation," as it's called, from your snowshoes than does snow that is more consolidated. There are female-specific snowshoes on the market, with the marketing hook being that they are narrower than normal 'shoes. Women, however, have told me that such adaptations are not necessary and that they have no trouble using normal snowshoes. Almost all snowshoers find it very useful to use ski poles when they are snowshoeing.

EMERGENCY SNOWSHOE REPAIR

Broken snowshoe frames can often be repaired with duct tape. Frames are usually broken by "bridging," which happens when a snowshoer tries to span any sort of opening in the snow—one of the most likely scenarios for bridging is crossing a fallen log by setting the forward tip of the snowshoe on the log while the back end of the 'shoe is still at a lower level on the snow.

Broken lacing on a snowshoe can be repaired with parachute cord or any other cordage of sufficient strength. Broken bindings can also be replaced with duct tape. It doesn't matter that much if your duct tape repair job results in some amount of tape protruding from the bottom of the snowshoe—unlike skis, you don't have to worry about a rough taping job interfering with your glide.

Another advantage of snowshoes is that it is possible for a person faced with a survival situation in the snow to fabricate snowshoes out of natural materials in the field. A flexible green limb can be twisted into a hoop and the two ends tied together to maintain the desired shape. A matching green limb can be tied into another hoop of similar size and shape

Snowshoes are an integral part of a winter enthusiast's repertoire.

Must-Have Survival Items

- [ ] Two quarts warm water
- [ ] Food
- [ ] At least one change of gloves, two pairs of mittens, Gore-Tex overmitts
- [ ] Change of socks
- [ ] Down jacket
- [ ] Spare hat
- [ ] Change of shirt
- [ ] Change of long underwear
- [ ] Two pairs of hand warmers
- [ ] Two headlamps and spare batteries
- [ ] Stove and fuel
- [ ] Waterproof matches and cigarette lighters
- [ ] Titanium kettle for melting snow
- [ ] Nylon tarp
- [ ] Shovel
- [ ] Thermarest pad
- [ ] Emergency blanket ("space blanket")
- [ ] Duct tape
- [ ] Grip ("kicker") wax and ski scraper
- [ ] Repair kit — parachute cord, screwdriver with interchangeable heads, spare ski pole basket, baling wire, steel wool, replacement ski tip
- [ ] Down booties
- [ ] At least one down sleeping bag for every two people in the party (even if you don't plan to camp out)

to balance the pair, and then each can be laced with parachute cord or some other rope. The cords can be twined around the outside of the limb, or, if you have a multipurpose knife with some sort of awl or drill, you could bore holes through the limb, insert the cordage, and tie it on the outside of the hoop.

If time and other circumstances permit, you can stiffen the green wood in snowshoes fabricated this way by slowly drying them in front of a fire. Of course you have to be careful to keep the 'shoes far enough away from the fire to prevent them from igniting, which probably calls for an extended period of vigilance while attending to both your fire and your snowshoes.

SNOWMOBILING

It seems to me that many people approach snowmobiling with an attitude of "Yippee! It's all fun and games!" The potential for fun and games is there, for sure, as is the element of useful winter transportation. But it's also true that snowmobiles are big, powerful machines with substantial potential for causing serious injury or death. The machines are also notorious for breaking down, which can leave a snowmobiler stranded in the snow—often many miles away from shelter or assistance.

A good beginning is to spend some time snowmobiling somewhat close to your base in order to gain some

Snowmobilers on tour in the Northern Rockies

level of proficiency with the machine before you head off into the remote backcountry. It's also important to carry at least a modicum of emergency repair parts and tools, and to know how to use them.

- ❑ Spare drive belt(s)

- ❑ Replacement spark plugs

- ❑ Shovel

- ❑ Block and tackle or come-along (for extricating stuck snow machine or righting an overturned machine)

- ❑ Tie-down straps

- ❑ Bungee cords (a generous number, preferably of various lengths)

- ❑ Engine oil

- ❑ Extra fuel

- ❑ Screwdrivers (at least one slotted and one Phillips, preferably with long shanks)

- ❑ Vise grips

- ❑ Large and small crescent wrenches

- ❑ Tow rope

- ❑ Saw, hatchet, or ax (for cutting logs out of the trail, or cutting trees on which your snowmobile may have become stuck, as by high centering)

It's also important to carry personal survival gear for yourself, beginning with appropriate snowmobiling clothing to keep you warm and dry in all snow conditions. A good quality helmet is a must, as is extra clothing in the event your machine breaks down somewhere out in the beyond and you have to spend some length of time marooned in the snow. Other important personal items include water (stowed in such a way as to prevent it from freezing), high-energy foods, a whistle, a signal mirror, a tarp, a compass with appropriate maps, and most important of all, fire-making materials. Fire is by far the most important element—with it, you can survive for quite some time without most or all of the other items. Without fire, there is a good chance you won't make it even if you have all the other items on the list.

Snowmobilers in falling snow, Madison Mountain Range, Montana

Additionally, it's important for snowmobilers to carry some means of moving around on deep snow in the event of a mechanical breakdown. I am often flabbergasted when I see people in my home area of southern Montana

Snowmobile stuck in the snow in front of a lodgepole pine forest, with no tools or survival gear visible

and northern Wyoming (and in other places I have visited) leaving on what appears to be extended snowmobile outings without snowshoes or cross-country skis. Snowshoes are easier to carry than cross-country skis, and they can be used with the boots that you already have on when snowmobiling.

CARRYING GEAR ON A SNOWMOBILE

Securing extra gear to a snowmobile can be a challenge. For strapping gear to a snowmobile, I prefer using bungee cords. They are superior to ropes because ropes can stretch and knots can loosen. Worse yet, ropes in general and knots in particular tend to clump up with snow and ice, and in that frozen condition can be next to impossible to untie.

I further make it a policy to use at least twice as many bungee cords as I think are necessary to tie my load down.

The author's snowmobile parked by a large snowdrift while on a sunrise photo outing. Note the snowshoes tied to the back of the seat.

Bungee cords can break, and their hooks can bend and give way. I remember one of the first snowmobile trips I ever took in my early days in Yellowstone National Park, in the winter of 1978–79. Along with my other gear on that trip, I hauled a pair of cross-country skis and a pair of ski poles. When I started to unload my snow machine at my destination, I found one of the poles was missing—it had come off somewhere along my 50-mile journey. Losing the pole in that case wasn't a disaster, as "all" I had to do was refuel my machine and retrace my route—for a distance of about 45 miles before I found the wayward pole.

But it's pretty easy to envision another scenario in which a missing ski pole could be a much bigger deal than just having to drive an extra 90 miles—where it could

The author's snowmobile and tow sled, after returning to the trailhead to find his pickup truck nearly buried in newly fallen snow

make the difference between living and dying. Using just one or two more bungee cords when I originally packed my load might have made the difference—in this case the difference between an extra two and a half hours on a snowmobile and a simple nonissue, where I could have enjoyed a relaxing evening visiting friends, which was the purpose of my trip in the first place.

Which leads me to another point: There is no place for carelessness in the outdoors, and that goes many times over for outdoor activities in the winter. In my own experience it seems that every single time I cut corners in any way, it inevitably comes back to haunt me. My observations of other people's actions have shown me the same thing. I absolutely hate having to think: "Damn it. I knew better, and I just didn't do what I know I should have done."

LONG-DISTANCE TRAVEL ON A SNOWMOBILE

Snowmobiles give you the capacity to travel very long distances into the backcountry within a short span of time. Traveling such long distances can lead to navigation problems, such as traveling so far you find yourself in unfamiliar country and might have a hard time finding your way back. Another frequent occurrence is people driving so far they run short of fuel or run out of daylight for their return trip. Even with GPS showing you the way back, it's unwise to travel cross-country in the dark, especially in mountainous terrain. GPS might show you the return route, but that straight line indication might lead you over a cliff or into avalanche terrain that you can't see in the dark.

Snowmobiler Walter Voeller uses a shovel to extricate a stuck snowmobile. Such a seemingly minor mishap can lead to a compounding chain of events that can leave a person in a dangerous situation.

SNOWMOBILES AND AVALANCHES

Another danger inherent with backcountry snowmobiling is from avalanches. Again, this is partly because snowmobiles can take you so far so fast that you can pass through a lot of varied terrain. Because of the machines' size, power, and noise, snowmobilers are also more likely than cross-country skiers or snowshoers to trigger a snowslide. If there is any chance whatsoever that you will encounter avalanche terrain on your snowmobile trip, it is imperative to be prepared for the danger. An avalanche beacon and avalanche shovel for each member of the group is a must. And each person has to remember to always keep his or her avalanche beacon on "send" mode while snowmobiling. Only after a slide has occurred and someone has been buried should the other members of the group switch their beacons to "receive" as they begin their search for the victim or victims.

An avalanche probe is another must. Probes are used to poke into the snow after an avalanche to search for buried victims. They look like long ski poles without baskets, and for economy of weight are often made of aluminum or carbon fiber. There are collapsible and telescoping models on the market; either is a good idea for snowmobilers because in their collapsed condition they are much easier to pack and carry on a snow machine.

A snow saw, even just a small one, is also a good idea. Saws can be used to cut down through the snowpack to reveal the various layers within the pack, and by examining them a knowledgeable person can glean some idea of how well the snow crystals are bonded to each other and therefore how likely they are to collapse and precipitate an avalanche. Snow saws are useful in other ways too, such as for cutting snow blocks to build an emergency shelter in case you have to spend one or more nights out in the backcountry.

The ability to recognize avalanche terrain is very important as well, as is at least a rudimentary knowledge of snow conditions and the potential ramifications of various sorts of snow and weather conditions. There are other pieces of avalanche-related equipment you can carry, such as streamers that can be affixed to a person's clothing, which hopefully will string out from an individual caught in a snowslide and help rescuers locate the buried individual. There are also flotation bags on the market, which fit around the neck and over the shoulders much like an inflatable life jacket for use on the water. The wearer can pull a rip cord similar to the rip cord on a parachute to inflate the bag in the event of an avalanche; the flotation properties of the air bag tend to keep a person caught in a slide on top of the snow as it rumbles downhill. Most important, the air bag will ideally leave the person deposited on top of the snow pile when the avalanche finally comes to a halt at the bottom of the slope.

Avalanches and the dangers they pose to winter recreationists will be discussed in more detail in the Avalanches chapter.

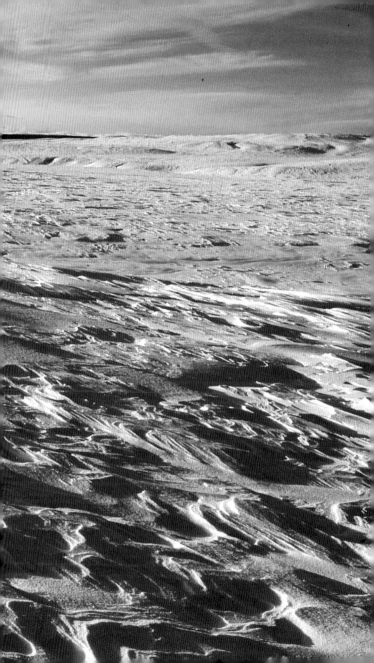

ROOF CLEARING

Many sections of both the United States and Canada receive so much snow that roof shoveling often becomes necessary. Problems stemming from snow and ice buildup on roofs fall into two basic categories: First is the obvious risk of having so much dead weight on a building that structural damage can occur. Structural damage from accumulated snow on a roof can range from relatively minor, such as broken eaves, to the complete collapse of a build-

ing. Even in the first scenario, repair bills can run into many thousands of dollars, to say nothing of the inconvenience involved, while the outright collapse of a structure can be financially catastrophic. And in the worst-case scenario, people might be inside the building when the roof comes down, with the possibility of death and serious injury to anyone unlucky enough to be caught under the cave-in.

A heavily laden building, badly in need of snow removal

The second is that water from melting snow on the roof of a heated building (such as homes and commercial structures) can back up behind ice dams along the eaves and then leak into the interior spaces.

Ice dams form along eaves when snow above the interior spaces of buildings is melted by heat percolating up through the roof. Meltwater then runs downhill under the snowpack on the roof, but when it flows onto the unheated eaves it refreezes into solid ice. Subsequent meltwater then has no place to go when it encounters the ice dam, so it backs up and can leak into the building. The best solution is to clear the entire roof so there is no more snow to melt into water and run down to the eaves.

I suppose that the roof shoveling work I have done all these years in Yellowstone is somewhat unique, but I do think that at least some of what I have learned is transferable to similar tasks in other parts of North America. Take, for example, someone who is clearing the

A gigantic, wind-deposited snow cornice on the edge of a roof in Yellowstone. Note the human figure at top right. Determining the edge of the roof is difficult but critical, so you won't be leveraged off the roof when the cornice falls.

roof of a hunting cabin somewhere in the North Woods, or shoveling structures at a seasonally closed resort anywhere that receives a lot of snow over the course of a long winter. Rangers and maintenance workers in parks and forests also have to clear government buildings in snow country, often in remote sections of seasonally isolated reserves.

HAZARDS IN ROOF CLEARING WORK

There are manifest hazards involved with working on a snow- and ice-covered roof, as well as others that might not come so readily to mind. First and foremost, of course, is the danger of falling. Another very real risk involves substantial amounts of snow falling from above, as from breaking cornices or avalanches from roof facets located above the one where a roof shoveler is working.

Many types of crampons are available that can be worn on the sole of your boots to provide traction on a snow- and ice-covered roof. Even more important than crampons, however, is good physical balance and a sense of confidence in what you are

Winter caretaker Dale Fowler straps ice crampons to his feet before climbing onto a steep, snow- and ice-covered roof.

doing. Taking short steps on a snow-covered roof is best, and you should absolutely never move without first looking to see that your foot will step onto a secure spot. *Always* look before you step.

You need to be confident about what you're doing while engaged in roof clearing work. That's especially true when you're wearing ice cleats or crampons. Time and again I have observed people who are tentative while moving around on a roof, and as a result they don't step down firmly and their crampons don't bite adequately. A further point about walking around on a snow-covered building: Good footing and good balance are more important considerations than is proximity to the edge of the roof.

I further hedge my bets in this regard by going around my buildings in the fall before the snows come to remove things like clotheslines, outdoor furniture, trash cans, and the like. Objects such as these could greatly increase the degree of injury you might suffer in a fall. I also put up my ladders in the fall and chain them to the eaves of the buildings. That way I don't have to worry about carrying or dragging ladders through several feet of snow in the middle of the winter, and because they are secured to the roof, I don't have to worry about them kicking out at ground level or sliding sideways on the eaves when I climb them.

Another danger involved with roof clearing is that sometimes there is so much snow that it's difficult to locate obstacles on the roof such as chimneys, vent pipes, or skylights. The first two can be tripping hazards, and I have read of cases where unfortunate shovelers walked onto snow-covered skylights and fell through, in some cases to

Using snowshoes to approach the roof of a building nearly buried in snow, Yellowstone National Park

their deaths. It can be especially difficult to locate the edge of the roof on the leeward side of a building, where snow overhangs and snow cornices form. I always approach such situations very cautiously, probing through the snow with a shovel or a snow saw to locate the eaves, and advancing only in short increments until I find the edge.

You also have to bear in mind that a cornice might break because of your disturbance—as big as they are, their bond to the roof can be quite fragile at times—and when it does break its massive weight overhanging the end of the building might leverage off a band of snow that extends some distance back from the edge of the roof. If you happen to be in the band of snow that cracks loose, you could quite possibly be leveraged right off the roof with the cornice. Such broken cornices tend to roll over in midair as they fall, and a person riding a cornice down might end up under the mass when it hits the ground. In addition to the clear danger of suffocating under such a load of snow, cornices are usually made out of dense, wind-packed snow that is so hard-frozen and heavy, a victim could be crushed outright even before suffocation occurs.

Risk of Avalanche

When working on a steep roof, say a roof with a pitch of about 35 degrees or more, avalanche danger is a consideration. This particular risk is often overlooked because of the fixation most people have on the danger of falling, but the danger of roof avalanche is very real and potentially deadly.

The first and probably the most important way to deal with avalanche danger is to learn about snow, and especially about snow crystals, which will give you clues as to how consolidated the snowpack is within itself, and also give you an idea of how firmly the snowpack is bonded to the roof of the building where you're working. Avalanches can occur when there is weakness in the snowpack in either area—a slab of snow can fracture and slide away, leaving a portion of the snowpack behind, or the entire snow load on a building can break loose all the way down to the shingles and leave just a bare roof behind after the snow slides off. Either case can bury a snow shoveler down below, which can lead to crushing or suffocation, especially if you are working alone.

I was unexpectedly caught in a roof avalanche on a roof near Old Faithful in Yellowstone National Park in March 1993. I was working with five friends on the roof of a large general store that is jammed with tourists in the

Pulling wire to cut snowpack loose from the roof of the closed general store at Old Faithful, Yellowstone National Park

summer but completely quiet and vacant in the winter. The building has a steep roof, probably in the neighborhood of 45 degrees, but I had already cleared that particular roof during seven previous winters, so I was experienced with the building. The roof was steep, but I never thought it could slide on its own because of the three dormers and six architectural valleys on the facet where we were working, design features that I thought would brace the snow slabs and hold them in place.

My strategy for clearing that particular building was (and still is) to shovel channels around the four principal slabs of snow between and beside the three dormers, and then to pull a slender wire under the slabs to cut them loose from the roof and precipitate my own avalanches in a controlled way. In 1993 we were just beginning to cut our trenches to isolate the four slabs of snow when I jammed a shovel blade under the snowpack to test the bond between the snowpack and the roof. My timing was perfect when I said to my companions, "I think it will go pretty easily this year." No sooner were the words out of my mouth than the snow from the entire roof—central slabs, dormers, valleys, everything—avalanched off.

All six of us were swept off the roof, and two were buried. Fortunately, both of the buried people were in an upright position, one guy buried up to his waist and another up to his neck, so both were able to communicate and, more important, able to breathe. The four of us who had been lucky enough to stay on top of the snow quickly dug out the other two, and I took a valuable lesson from the episode: Never, *never* put yourself in the danger zone where you might get caught in an avalanche, at least in a roof clearing situation, no matter what you think the avalanche conditions might or might not be.

By way of illustrating the danger, I did some calculations on the amount of weight that slid off the roof during that incident. The roof surface that slid is about 5,000 square feet, and the average load on the roof at that time was about 100 pounds per square foot (the snowpack on the building averaged 5 to 6 feet deep at the time of the avalanche). A little arithmetic shows that about a half million pounds of snow avalanched from the roof of the general store that day—more than enough weight to do a lot of damage to anyone caught underneath it.

I don't think roping up on an avalanche-prone roof is the answer: Being tethered to the ridge of the roof by a rope and a climbing harness would be a very bad idea in the event of a snowslide. At the very least you would get badly pummeled, and at worst you might be fatally crushed—it probably would be something like being tethered under a cascading waterfall. Instead, my response has been to continue to clear the same avalanche-prone roofs for which I am responsible, but to do so by starting from the edge or the top of the roof, never placing myself in a position where I might get caught if the roof unexpectedly gives way and slides.

In climates that are snowy and cold, snowpack can go through many months of metamorphosis before the spring melt begins. The result is that the snow continues to settle and compact, and by mid- to late winter can become unbelievably dense and hard. I have calculated weights of more than 160 pounds of snowpack per square foot on the surfaces of roofs I clear. That's a lot of weight—160 pounds per square foot means that one 4×8 sheet of plywood is holding up well over 5,000 pounds of snow.

Risk of Snow Falling from Above

My favorite technique for clearing snow off roofs is to use an old-fashioned crosscut saw to cut the snowpack into manageable blocks, which I then balance on a shovel blade to skid off the roof. A typical block of snow is about 5 or 6 square feet at its base, so a little arithmetic shows that just one block can weigh 500 to 1,000 pounds. The point of all this is not just that the blocks are heavy, which they are, but also that the snow is so hardpacked the blocks can be a very real hazard if they topple over on you. Because the

Jenny Wolfe saws deep snow-pack into manageable cubes, roof clearing work in Yellowstone National Park.

blocks are so hard, they will not disintegrate if they fall over and hit you. Instead they hit with impact, and with all that weight behind them they could very easily blow out a knee, break a foot, or worse. I often compare manipulating snow blocks around on a roof and the toppling hazard they present to trying to move an upright chunk of a tree while balancing it on a shovel blade.

I usually work alone when I am clearing roofs. I enjoy the solitude, and use the time for thinking and reflecting. Is it dangerous to work alone? It can be; there are scenarios where having a partner could make the difference between life and death. And remember that I have many years of experience and am able to recognize potential danger. On the other hand, when working with someone else, it's important to focus on the task at hand and not lose concentration talking to each other or, worse, horsing around. Avoiding an accident in the first place is much better than any solution to an injury after it has occurred.

It also doesn't hurt to let someone know where you are going and approximately when you expect to return.

The author balances a tall and heavy snow block on a shovel, working shirtless in warm and sunny winter weather.

Be clear that you prefer some flexibility, to allow for some leeway. If you go off to shovel a roof in a remote and quiet area, you could decide that the setting is so beautiful you want to go for a ski before you head home. Or maybe the location is so inviting that you choose to camp overnight so you can wake to see the sun at that magical moment when it rises over the horizon. If you've asked for 12 to 15 hours' leeway, they won't worry and you can have a wonderful experience, but you can expect help if you need it.

Personally, I enjoy the freedom to get away by myself, but safety is paramount. And experience is the best way to build up that safety cushion.

AVALANCHES

Avalanches pose a clear and potentially overpowering danger to any winter enthusiast who ventures into terrain where snowslides can occur.

Other than comparatively small avalanches that have slid off buildings, such as the one I described in the chapter on roof clearing work, I have never been caught in a snowslide. Nor have I ever directly witnessed anything more than small to moderate slides while out in the mountains.

The awesome leavings of an avalanche in the following summer, after all the snow has melted away. ERIC KNOFF

I have, however, had three friends killed in snow avalanches, and many times I have come across the awesome aftermath of massive slides.

One was in the Beartooth Mountains of southern Montana in September 2005. It obviously had happened sometime during the previous winter, and it had taken until autumn for all the snow the avalanche piled up at the bottom of the slope to melt away. It was fascinating to see spring flowers like spring beauties and glacier lilies blooming at the site in September, but the big banks of avalanched snow had only recently melted, and in effect spring had just come to that particular spot.

The other slide that sticks in my memory was even more impressive. I came across its colossal remains in September 1997 while hiking with a companion up Sunlight Creek in northwestern Wyoming. We passed several large slides where unmelted snow was still piled on the old mining road we were walking along. But then we came to an avalanche chute where a truly tremendous slide had come off the north-facing slope above the creek. The slide had scoured the slope above us clean of boulders and downed logs. It also had ripped all living trees out of its path, and all that debris—massive amounts of still-unmelted snow and ice mixed with logs, boulders, and broken but still green coniferous trees, all of it jackstrawed together— was piled across the road, and was still 30 to 40 feet deep under our feet.

The stupendous avalanche had roared all the way down to the creek below us, of course, and it was also evident that its mass and momentum had carried the toe of the slide a considerable distance up the opposing slope on the other side of the stream. And this was in September, after a full summer of melting must have greatly reduced the original footprint of the slide. The purpose of our hike was to scout the trails in the area for a potential horse trip later in the fall, but because of the avalanched obstructions we decided against the idea. I remember joking that it would have been easier to storm a wartime barricade with an old-fashioned cavalry charge than it would have been to cross those chaotically tangled, slippery debris fields with riding horses and a packstring.

But seriously, and without question, any living creature unlucky enough to be in front of such a force would have been doomed, and because of this and other observations I have come to the firm conclusion that the only sure way to avoid getting caught and quite possibly killed in an avalanche is to never venture into avalanche terrain in the first place. There must be no more horrifying feeling than to be below a snowfield that breaks loose and inexorably begins to slide toward you, quickly gaining speed and volume as it rushes downhill, and then to come to the awful realization that inevitably you are going to be caught up in its roiling white mass.

AWESOME POWER OF AVALANCHES

It's hard to overstate the potential power engendered by the mass and speed of avalanching snow. According to some sources, there have been avalanches as large as 1 million cubic yards of snow, and they sometimes reach speeds of 300 miles per hour. A research project in the

Swiss Alps determined that the pressure of one incoming avalanche reached 11 tons per square foot, while another group of researchers working in another area of Switzerland found that the avalanche they evaluated generated "only" 500 pounds of pressure per square foot, but the force of that slide was sufficient to topple and tumble a locomotive. And you don't even have to be hit by the avalanching snow itself to suffer great impact—the force of the air displaced by so much snow sliding downhill so fast can be enough to blast apart almost anything in its way. Even strongly engineered highways and railroads and stoutly constructed buildings have virtually exploded in front of "avalanche wind," as the surge of air in front of the cascading snow is called.

Here's a tidbit to illustrate the danger posed by avalanches to winter travelers: In my home area in and around Yellowstone, since the park's creation in 1872, far more people have died in avalanches than have been killed by the park's famous bears.

All that said, most winter enthusiasts will find themselves in avalanche terrain at some point in their outdoor careers, and therefore it behooves them to learn as much as possible about the phenomenon. The truth is, most winter recreationists ignore the threat of avalanches, at least to some extent and from time to time, and venture onto steep and snowy terrain in the interest of fun and thrill seeking—or sometimes simply as a matter of "saving time" by taking the more direct but also more treacherous route.

Avalanches come in two fundamental types. The first is a slab avalanche, where a weakness within the snowpack gives way and allows an overlying layer or layers of snow to slide over a base layer that remains bonded to the ground and therefore does not release and avalanche along with the upper strata. The second type is sometimes called a climax avalanche, which involves all the snow on a slope down to ground level releasing and sliding away. The second type involves the release of more snow, of course, and can be considered the more deadly, but many slab avalanches are breathtaking in size and more than sufficient to bury and kill anyone who happens to be in the way.

That said, always bear in mind that it doesn't take a very big slide to bury you, as getting buried even to a shallow level is all that's necessary to lead to fatal results. Beyond that, avalanche danger can sometimes pop up where you might not expect it. For instance, the closest I ever came to getting caught in an avalanche was in April 1983. I was working for the National Park Service at the time, in the ranger division in Yellowstone. I was assigned to patrol the Blacktail Plateau area in the northern part of the park, specifically to watch for elk antler poachers. One day I decided to climb a small, unnamed butte to get a better view of the surrounding country. Blacktail Plateau is comparatively low in relation to most of Yellowstone and therefore doesn't receive nearly as much snow as most of the rest of the park. On top of that, it was springtime and most of the snow in the immediate area had already melted, and I just wasn't thinking of avalanche danger.

As I was climbing the side of the butte, I came to a relatively small snowfield that was the remnant of a drift that had formed during the previous winter. The field was small only in a relative sense—it covered an area probably at least the size of a baseball infield, maybe twice that large. As I was climbing over the snow, I began to posthole, or punch through the snow with my feet with each step I took. When I was partway up the steeply sloping snowfield, my postholing caused it to collapse around me, but for some reason it did not slide after it collapsed—even though the slope was steep enough to slide under the right conditions. I was alone, so if conditions had been just a little bit different that could well have been the end of my story right there.

ASSESSING AVALANCHE DANGER

Terrain is the most important consideration in judging avalanche potential. Because of prevailing winds, in most areas north- and east-facing slopes accumulate much more snow than do south- and west-facing aspects.

Leeward slopes not only accumulate deeper snowpacks but also tend to develop snow cornices (overhanging edges of snow), especially along ridge crests at the top of the slopes. Snow cornices can be and often are gigantic. On some of the higher mountains in my home area, these frozen waves of wind-packed snow can be the width and depth of basketball arenas and extend for hundreds of yards in length. Cornices are interesting in that for all their enormous size and weight they can sometimes be held in place by only the most fragile bond, and only a slight disturbance is needed to tip the balance and break them loose.

The breaking of a large cornice can precipitate a major avalanche with potentially catastrophic consequences for anyone who happens to be below. Not only is the snow in the cornice itself apt to continue its slide down the slope below, but its impact can also break loose the snowpack on the slope where it lands, thus adding its mass to a slide that enlarges as it goes.

Calculating the degree of slope is of paramount importance when evaluating avalanche terrain. Slopes shallower than 25 degrees rarely avalanche for the obvious reason that such slopes just aren't steep enough to slide. But always remember that there can be steeper, more avalanche-prone slopes somewhere above the shallow slopes in your immediate view. The momentum of slides originating on steeper

Avalanche researcher inspects the fracture line at the crown of an avalanche that has slid. ERIC KNOFF

slopes above can carry across shallower slopes that might not avalanche on their own.

Very steep slopes (over 60 degrees) also rarely avalanche as they are so steep that insufficient snow accumulates there—instead most falling snow simply sifts downhill and builds up at the bottom of the hill. Cornices can still develop at the crowns of such slopes, however, even those as steep as 90 degrees, and they can break and fall on anything below.

Slopes most likely to avalanche are those between 30 and 45 degrees. Those slopes have the potential to hold snow for a time as it accumulates, but then as conditions change those loaded slopes can give way and send their accumulated snow cascading downhill. As a general rule of thumb, consider that a 25-degree slope is comparable to a beginner's ski run at a downhill ski resort. A slope of about 30 degrees is considered an intermediate run, 35 degrees equates to an expert slope, and 40 to 45 degrees is classified as a double black diamond. If you really want to be technical, however, you can use a compass or a slope meter to be exact. Some sources say that you need to be that precise in your evaluation of the grade, that just a degree or two difference in slope can make the difference in whether a given slope will slide. But in my mind if it's that critical to evaluate the degree of slope so exactly, then things are just too touchy to risk playing on or traversing across such avalanche terrain in the first place.

Vegetated slopes are less likely to avalanche than are bare hillsides. But sometimes avalanches are so big and so powerful they simply smash through anything in their path, picking up rocks and boulders and even ripping out or breaking off trees up to many feet in diameter. This sort of avalanche is especially dangerous, as the churning debris mixed with the sliding snow increases the lethality of the event. Getting caught in this sort of slide would be similar to being tossed around in a tsunami wave, I suppose, and taking a battering from the flotsam in the turbulent water—only the avalanche scenario would probably be worse than the tsunami.

I had a friend who died in just this sort of avalanche on Mount Norris in Yellowstone National Park. On February 21, 1992, mountain lion researcher Greg Felzein was caught in a fairly small slide and killed by head trauma from rocks in the slide as he was carried along by the avalanche. In Felzein's case he was buried at such a shallow level when the avalanche came to a halt that he possibly could have simply stood up out of the snow had he still been OK. But the fact that he was face down in the snow and there was no vapor mask of frozen exhalations in front of his face indicated that he was not breathing and probably was dead when his body came to rest at the bottom of the slide.

Another factor to consider is the shape of the hillside above you. Hanging basins, or "bowls," as mountaineering enthusiasts like to call them, can be especially dangerous because when they do slide, all the snow in the bowl can be funneled to the basin's outlet. The funneling effect concentrates the sliding snow in the neck of the outlet, so even a relatively small slide can turn into a deadly force if you happen to be caught in this sort of constricting landform, which avalanche experts like to call a "terrain trap." This sort of terrain feature was a factor in Greg Felzein's death.

In addition to the danger presented by funneling landforms, it's also possible for an avalanche to come down from so far above that you can't even see its starting point. I have seen the aftermath of slides that began near the very tops of mountains, which gathered so much additional snow and momentum as they slid that their inertia carried them far below the elevation where there was enough local snow to precipitate an avalanche. In this sort of scenario, it might be possible to be skiing or even hiking at such a low elevation that you would be in little or no snow and have little concern for the danger of avalanche, but then be caught in the lower reaches of a slide.

I saw the signs of just such a slide along a little stream near Emigrant Peak in the Absaroka Mountain Range of southern Montana once. That particular slide had picked up so much momentum that it carried down out of the forest (carrying massive amounts of broken forest debris with it) and almost to the level of the semiarid sagebrush grassland. I saw the same sort of phenomenon in several places along the Going-to-the-Sun Road in Glacier National Park on a ski trip in March 1998.

AVALANCHE TRIGGERS

Factors like degree of slope, compass aspect, density of vegetation, and landform configuration all determine whether a given slope *can* slide. It is snow conditions and degree of disturbance that determine whether an avalanche *will* happen at a specific point in time.

So in addition to paying attention to landscape details like slope, compass aspect, and landform features, you have to know something about snow and snow crystals to form an idea of what the avalanche danger is at a given time. The properties of snow crystals depend on the weather conditions when they originally fell, as well as the weather conditions during the whole time they have been lying on the ground. What matters is how well they are bonded to each other, and how well the snow crystals at the very bottom of the snowpack are bonded to the ground. Ideally, all winter enthusiasts should learn all they can about snow and then apply what they know by digging snow test pits in the area where they intend to travel or recreate. Looking at the various levels in the snow and the bonding characteristics in each level can give you some idea of how likely it is that the snow will break loose and slide.

A snow saw—preferably a small one made for cutting small blocks for building snow shelters, and therefore easy to carry—can be useful in digging your snow evaluation pit. A saw makes it easier to dig a pit with vertical sides where the layers in the snow are more clearly exposed. There are also pocket cards you can purchase and carry that give you pointers on what to look for in the snow for clues to avalanche conditions. It's actually fun to dig snow pits and look at the layers revealed on the sides—in a very real sense the history of the entire winter is exposed to you on the walls of your pit.

Simply put, what you are trying to evaluate in your snow pit is whether the cohesiveness and structural strength in the snowpack is adequate to hold the load that has been placed upon it. Many factors can create a zone of weakness in the snow, but an easy way to identify a weak layer is with a finger test. Just poke a finger or fingers, or even a whole fist or elbow, into the various layers of the snow to determine how consolidated it is. Obviously, the larger the number of fingers you can poke into a layer the less consolidated and weaker it is—if you can punch a whole fist or an elbow into a layer of coarsely grained, crumbly snow, then it's really weak. A red flag is when you have hard, consolidated layers above a zone of more weakly bonded snow. The weaker layer can collapse under the weight of the snow above, and then the consolidated mass overlying the weak zone can begin to move as a unit and precipitate an avalanche.

Other red flags that you can spot are the signs of avalanches that have recently slid. Cracks in the snow are another warning signal, as is the appearance of large amounts of recently deposited snow in the form of either freshly fallen snow or windblown deposits. Such additional loading may overwhelm the snowpack's ability to hold fast to the mountainside or to the layers of older snow below. Hollow sounds underfoot, and especially hollow sensations that can be felt with a ski pole or other probe, are another sign of weakness. Snowfields collapsing around you, a phenomenon often accompanied by ominous "whumping" sounds, are especially scary. Free-flowing water either within or at the base of the snowpack, as occurs in late winter and spring, is another big-time warning sign. Instead of red flags, it might be better to call these avalanche danger indications red lights—if you detect such warning signals, it probably would be a good

Striations on the surface of snowpack indicate meltwater is running somewhere under the surface—a warning sign that avalanche danger is high.

idea to stop and find someplace else to spend your day that's altogether away from the danger of avalanche.

I remember hunting elk in the Gallatin Mountains of southern Montana in December 1993. I was out with my father and one of his friends, and there was a lot of snow for so early in the season. Because my dad's friend was new to the country, we decided he would go with me while my dad went off alone. Within a very short time it became apparent that snow conditions were extremely treacherous that day—snow layers around my dad's friend and me collapsed with that scary whumping sound more times than we could even count, and I made sure that he and I stayed well away from any slopes that might slide after their snow layers collapsed.

My dad, on the other hand, has always been more than gung ho when it comes to hunting, and he not only ventured into yet higher country where there was even more snow, but he also chanced going out on steeper slopes. Long story short, he ended up being swept into a considerable avalanche and saved himself by grasping an overhead tree limb as he was being carried along. Even so, he wound up buried to his waist, from where he couldn't extricate himself until he unloaded his rifle and then used its butt as a shovel to dig himself out. My dad did not return to the trailhead until long after dark—a cause of much worry for me and my dad's friend—and when he did return, it was in a state of extreme chill and exhaustion. Red lights, indeed.

PREDICTABILITY AND UNPREDICTABILITY OF AVALANCHES

My dad was lucky that day, and his friend and I were fortunate that we were able to recognize the avalanche danger and adjust our activities accordingly, but no matter how much you know about snow and no matter how well schooled you might be in evaluating avalanche conditions, it's impossible to be correct 100 percent of the time with your avalanche predictions.

Unquestionably there are many people who know more about snow conditions and avalanche forecasting than I do. But it's also true that it's quite common to read about incidents where buildings and highways have been blown away by the avalanche beast, even though the structures were supposedly engineered to withstand a slide of any magnitude. Entire towns, or at least portions thereof, have been wiped out—though the towns had been constructed on sites determined by experts to be locations where avalanches never run.

Beyond that, it is even more common to read or otherwise hear about avalanche experts who are killed by snowslides while out evaluating the risk, or while they are working to reduce the danger by using explosives to blast loose accumulated snow before it breaks loose at some unforeseen time and slides down on unsuspecting people below. It's not that uncommon even to read about academicians getting caught in fatal slides while out doing research in their snowy fields of study. I am often moved to think about an old German folk riddle: "What flies without wings, claws without hands, and sees without eyes?" The answer is, of course, the avalanche creature.

If you have to venture into avalanche terrain, you should first thoroughly evaluate the situation as I have outlined above. Next, you should not venture into avalanche terrain alone—and this is coming from someone who really likes to venture out alone in almost all other circumstances. Everyone in your party should have appropriate avalanche equipment, which as a minimum includes an avalanche shovel, an avalanche probe, and a transceiver. Ideally, everyone in your party will know something about snow and avalanche danger, and the group will have engaged in discussions about the danger and possible scenarios ahead of time.

There are other avalanche-related safety accoutrements, some of which were discussed in the Snowmobiling chapter. Beyond equipping yourselves correctly, you should make sure that everyone in your group has his or her avalanche beacon set on "send" as you travel; only after an avalanche has occurred and someone has been buried should the other members of the party switch their transceivers to "receive." Practicing with your avalanche beacons ahead of time is a very good idea too. You don't have to bury a living person to practice locating a transceiver—you can just bury the transceiver itself and then search for it by locating the signal it sends out.

When crossing dangerous slopes, only one person at a time should be exposed to the danger. This point applies no matter how you're traveling, whether by ski, snowshoe, or snowmobile.

While that person is traversing the danger zone, the other members of the party should be vigilant in watching for signs of a developing avalanche, such as cracks appearing in the snow or ominous cracking or collapsing sounds emanating from the snow. If the dreadful event happens and the snow begins to move, members of the party who are off to the side should do the best they can to keep the victim in sight, and above all memorize and, as precisely as possible, mark the place where the victim was last seen.

And always remember, just because one or several members of the party have traversed the danger zone and the snow hasn't slid doesn't mean that the next person won't set off an avalanche. Many times I have skied as part of a group across snowfields and observed the snow layers collapse upon the passage of the second or fifth or eighth person in line—this after the strata held during the passage of the first several people. But in keeping with my view that the only way to be entirely safe with avalanches is to avoid avalanche country altogether, all those instances happened on low-angle, non-avalanche terrain. No snow broke loose and slid, and no one was hurt.

SURVIVING AN AVALANCHE

If the unthinkable happens and you are caught in an avalanche, the best thing to do is to try to swim with it, as you might do if caught in a powerful river current. Try to swim toward the edge of the slide as it is moving along, especially toward the outside of a curve in the flow or on an angle toward a shallower slope. Also try to swim upward toward the surface to keep yourself on top of the sliding

A large avalanche in progress. ERIC KNOFF

snow. If possible, try to grab an overhanging limb or some other anchor to pull yourself out of the avalanche.

When the snow comes to a halt, it will set up as hard as the proverbial concrete—it really does—and if you are below the surface when you feel the slide slowing, cup your hands over your mouth and nose to form a small air pocket. Doing so will keep powder snow from packing into your throat and nostrils, and will also leave you with a little breathing pocket if you are left submersed.

It's usually not worthwhile to yell for your rescuers if you are buried—sound does not travel well through snow. It's better to save your breath unless you can tell that searchers are very close. Some sources suggest spitting and watching which way your saliva drips as a way to determine which way is up. That probably helps only in the

Snowy rubble left in the aftermath of a major avalanche. ERIC KNOFF

unlikely event that your hands are free enough to allow you to begin to dig your own way up and out.

Other members of the party who have remained on top of the snow must work fast. Realistically, the chances of rescue are only about one in three for anyone who is fully buried, and that small chance declines rapidly as time goes on—after a period of only about 30 minutes, the chance of pulling out an entombed victim alive falls to near zero. Another point to bear in mind is that if you give up on an immediate search for a buried victim and go for help, by the time you return you almost certainly will be working to recover a body rather than rescue a live person.

The first thing rescuers must do is determine whether it is safe to venture onto the avalanched snow. If so, there should be a quick conference to determine a plan of action and to designate a role for each member of the rescue party. If anyone in the group has a fix on where the victim came to a stop, that obviously should be the first place to look. Telltale signs in the snow—things like skis or poles, items of clothing, a part of the snowmobile that the victim was riding at the time of the slide, or anything else that offers a clue as to where the person might be buried—are the next key. If nothing of this sort is present, the next step is to look in likely places of deposition such as the outside curves of the avalanche, tree wells, or the lower toe of the slide. If rescuers have no luck finding the person in any of those places, a systematic search in a thorough, geometric pattern should begin.

A dog can be very useful if one is present, especially if the dog is trained in search and rescue work. Even if not trained, most dogs are naturally inclined to look for

a missing person, and at least in some situations a dog's sense of smell is superior to any modern technology people can bring to the scene.

Ranger Bob Duff with search and rescue–trained dog Hoss on a snowmobile near Madison Junction, Yellowstone National Park

Searchers should fan out but stay close enough to each other that they won't miss a buried victim in between their paths. Everyone in the group should have an avalanche transceiver, which was carried on "send" mode until the time of the accident, and which members of the rescue group switch to "receive" upon beginning the search. Everyone in the group should also have an avalanche probe, which is used to probe through the snow to find the buried person. Probing intervals must be tight enough to locate the victim, regardless of the position of his or her body—remember that the victim might be buried in an upright posture, and therefore the part of the body that might be located by probing will be smaller than that of someone buried in a horizontal position. Everyone in the party should also have a shovel to use in the hoped-for event that the victim is located.

Mark each area when searched so duplication of effort and loss of time do not occur during the search. If there are enough people present, it's a good idea to post a lookout to watch for any development that might pose a danger to the searchers. The lookout can also continue scanning the avalanche field for clues that might have been missed during the initial pass over the scene.

Again, if there are enough rescuers present, another person can be assigned to set up a first-aid/warm-up station. Ideally this station will be in a safe, somewhat level location. Depending on circumstances, this assignment can involve putting up some sort of wind protection—a tarp or a tent. Building a fire at the site is also a good idea, so proximity to fuel as well as shelter from the wind are both considerations. Depending again on the number of people present and other considerations, such as how far you are from help, one person might be dispatched to summon additional help. You may have to dispense with some of the steps and assignments outlined above if there aren't enough rescuers to do them all—circumstances and common sense will dictate priorities—but always bear in mind that time is of the absolute essence.

Hopefully the victim will be found and extricated alive, although about a third of avalanche victims die from trauma suffered during the slide itself, and therefore are beyond saving no matter how prompt and efficient the rescue effort. Even if the victim is alive when found, he or she will be chilled, frightened, and perhaps suffering from non-fatal injuries sustained in the slide. At that point the person should be transported to the first-aid and warming station, where wounds and other issues can be treated, the victim can be warmed up, and the whole party can regroup.

ERIC KNOFF

BLIZZARDS, FROSTBITE, AND HYPOTHERMIA

The National Weather Service defines a blizzard as a snowstorm with winds of at least 35 miles per hour, with enough blowing snow that visibility is reduced to a quarter mile or less, and which lasts for at least 3 hours. A severe blizzard is further defined as a storm with winds of at least 45 miles per hour resulting in near zero visibility and temperatures of 10°F or lower.

Gathering storm in an open valley in very cold conditions, northern Rocky Mountains

The combination of strong wind, reduced visibility, and strong cold makes for an obvious danger to human welfare and even survival. In my mind the biggest threat comes from the reduced visibility—you can deal with almost anything as long as you can see what you're doing. And beyond that, I believe that it's not the blizzard that's dangerous, or the avalanche, or any other snow event. It's the lack of knowledge in how to deal with the event that is the real danger. To survive a blizzard, you must first get out of the blizzard, seek or construct some sort of shelter, and keep yourself warm, dry, hydrated, and well fed.

STRANDED IN A VEHICLE

In today's world it's probably much more likely you will be caught in a blizzard while driving in your car than in the backcountry. As with just about everything else, preparing ahead of time is the key. It's a good idea to have winter survival gear like a shovel, tire chains, a tow chain or rope, a full tank of fuel, and fuel line antifreeze for your vehicle. The list of personal items for yourself should include a sleeping bag or blankets, extra clothing, stout work gloves, and food and water. Flashlights and/or headlamps and perhaps some extra batteries are good things to have too.

It's a really good idea to have at least a few chemical hand warmers on board as well. No matter what gear you have along when a wintry emergency strikes, it won't do you any good if your hands and fingers are too cold to use it. Just a couple of hand warmers can restore the dexterity you need to do what has to be done, and in a very real sense can make all the difference between surviving and perishing, or at least between relative comfort and misery. Employing hand warmers to warm other parts of the body often works well too. You can place them anywhere close to your body, where they provide a nice increase in warmth to your metabolic equation. This is especially true if you are wrapped in blankets or a sleeping bag that will hold the heat close to you.

Most sources stress that you should not leave your vehicle if stranded in a winter storm. I agree that is usually good advice, but there are times when common sense should come into play as well. There are many accounts of people fatally losing their way in the blowing snow of a blizzard, of course, but there are also accounts of other people who remained in their cars and died there from the cold or from dehydration and hunger. If you are caught in a remote area where the chances of being found are small, then at some point you will have to weigh the risk of trying to stick it out in your vehicle compared to your chances of walking (or skiing or snowshoeing) back home, or someplace where you can find help. Only you, based on your experience and your take of the circumstances at the time, can make that decision.

While you are stuck in the snow, run your vehicle's engine sparingly—perhaps 10 minutes per hour. Use your shovel to clear the snow from your exhaust pipe each time before you turn on your engine to make sure you don't asphyxiate yourself with fumes. Crack your windows a little to allow air inflow, again to guard against asphyxiation. Use this heat interval to warm not only yourself but also your water and food, to keep them from freezing. For best results, place your food and water immediately in front of one of your vehicle's heat vents.

Exercise as much as you can without breaking a sweat, both to keep yourself warm and to keep yourself supple and alert. You can exercise to some extent inside your vehicle by doing things like leg stretches, foot flexes, and the like. Or you can get out of the car and walk around too, as long as you don't get so far away you risk losing sight of the vehicle and cannot find your way back. The important thing to remember is to not overdo it and get wet from sweat—getting wet while stranded in a winter storm will be cold and uncomfortable, if not fatal.

Play some sort of game, like a word game, or use whatever gaming accessories you might have on hand to keep yourself cheerful and alert. If you have a companion or companions, you also might want to consider sleeping in shifts so that you don't go to sleep and never wake up, as apparently happens to some people when they freeze to death. Absolutely never allow yourself to fall asleep while your vehicle is idling. At the very least, you will end up burning a lot of your precious fuel, and at worst there's a good chance you will die in your sleep from carbon monoxide poisoning from your vehicle's exhaust. Because your survival might depend on cooperation and division of labor, make every effort to get along with your companions—don't play the blame game by accusing someone in your party of being at fault for your predicament.

Cell phones and other electronic gadgets are not necessarily reliable during blizzards, nor in hurricanes or wildfires. Heavy amounts of falling or blowing snow often block cell phone signals, and batteries do not perform or last well in cold weather.

BACKCOUNTRY BLIZZARDS

If you are caught in a blizzard while in the backcountry, you obviously will not have the luxury of the ready shelter of an enclosed motor vehicle, and shelter is, of course, one of the most pressing needs in cold, windy weather. If you cannot get home, seek out some sort of naturally sheltered spot before the blizzard hits, someplace like a stand of forest or a wind-protected landform. Knowing the weather forecast for the area where you are going to be traveling or recreating is helpful in this regard. It's even more important to know how to read the weather yourself while you are in the backcountry. If you can see a blizzard coming,

Cross-country skier Louise Mercier looks at an approaching blizzard on back track, skiing across Shoshone Lake, Yellowstone National Park

A backcountry shelter fabricated from the materials at hand, Madison Mountain Range, southern Montana. JERRY BREKKE

or somehow otherwise know that its arrival is imminent, it's time to head for the most sheltered spot you can find. If you are caught out in the open during a severe blizzard, and you can't find or make your way to some sort of structural shelter, you might have to resort to building a shelter out of snow or digging a snow cave or a snow trench shelter.

I was out in the foothills of the Absaroka Mountains near my home in southern Montana once when I saw a front of windy and snowy weather coming toward me. Because of the open nature of that part of the upper Yellowstone River Valley, I was able to see the storm coming from a long distance away, but I was so far out on an exposed hillside that I wasn't able to make it to cover before the blizzard hit. The slope where I was hiking was vegetated only with grass and sagebrush, so I started for a north-facing and timbered slope a mile or so away. Because the bare hillside was steep and already snow covered, the going was slow, so I didn't make it off the slippery slope before the blizzard hit. The wind hit with such force that I couldn't stand upright, and there was so much falling and blowing snow I couldn't see much either. All I could do for some period of time was crouch down and wait.

Fortunately there was a slight lull in the storm after a while, and I was able to see well enough to continue moving toward the north-facing slope. Still, the wind was so strong I couldn't stand upright and walk in a normal fashion. Instead I had to scuttle along like a crab, keeping my profile low to the ground and using my hands to steady myself by grasping exposed rocks and tufts of sagebrush as I moved along. I finally managed to reach the ridge crest between the exposed slope where the blizzard caught me and the timbered slope I had chosen as my refuge, and as soon as I dropped over the edge into the forest I was almost completely out of the wind. From there I was able to configure my route to take advantage of cover—in this case timbered hillsides and watercourses—and stay out of the worst of the wind all the way back home.

I include this anecdote to show how valuable timber and terrain features can be as wind protection. On even the windiest day, it's usually possible to find someplace in the woods, or in some sort of sheltered draw or other landscape feature, where the wind is either largely or completely absent.

Complete loss of visibility is frightening and hard to imagine until you have experienced it yourself. A good friend of mine, the famous bear biologist Chuck Jonkel of Missoula, Montana, spent over forty years studying polar bears on and around Hudson Bay. Chuck passed away in 2016, but he liked to tell the story of how he was once holed up during a fierce blizzard in the town of Baker Lake, Nunavut, on the northwestern side of Hudson Bay. The storm persisted for several days, by which time Chuck was feeling cooped up and wanted to get outside for a little walk. Even though he was already quite experienced in the Arctic, Chuck was surprised by the force of the wind and almost total lack of visibility resulting from the blowing snow, which obscured the buildings and almost everything else in town. He continued his walk, however, until he collided head on with the wall of a building he hadn't even seen until he smashed his face into it.

By feeling the building with his hands and catching glimpses of it during brief lulls in the wind, Chuck was finally able to identify the structure—as a building not only at the very edge of town but also on the *exact opposite side of the town* from where he thought he was. If Chuck hadn't blindly collided with that building, he would have continued stumbling out onto the open tundra beyond the edge of town, where he surely would have perished. As a response to his close call, from that point forward Chuck made it a practice to string ropes between structures in his Arctic camps, which people could hang onto for guidance as they made their way from one place to another.

Blizzards obscure visibility not only by filling the air with blowing snow, but also by blowing snow into your face and eyes. Even cold, dry snow tends to melt a little when it hits the warmth and moisture of your eyes, after which it sticks on your eyelids and lashes, making it difficult to see as well as being cold. In wintry weather, especially in cold and windy weather, the snow on your eyes can freeze in place and then be really hard to remove—many times I have had to hold a bare hand over my eyes for some period of time to melt snow crusted on them before I could wipe it away.

Goggles, often called glacier goggles, are a good solution to this problem. But I perspire heavily, so I find fogging to be a problem when I wear goggles, even during very cold weather, so if you're like me you might opt for a pair of good quality wraparound sunglasses that afford a high degree of eye protection from blowing snow but still allow for some air circulation behind the lenses so that perspired vapor can evaporate. Sunglasses with a strap that wraps around the back of the head will keep the glasses from falling off when you bend over or from blowing off in strong winds.

With either goggles or sunglasses, your vision in snow and low light can be enhanced by using colored lenses in the orange to yellow range. Clear lenses are a good idea for nighttime travel or recreation—even if it's not blizzarding, clear lenses can protect your eyes from dangers that you can't see in the dark, such as overhanging limbs.

FROSTBITE AND HYPOTHERMIA

Severe windchills engendered by the cold air and strong winds of a blizzard can lead to frostbite and hypothermia. Windchill can be described as the "real-feel" temperature of cold air combined with wind (see Windchill

Chart). Frostbite is the freezing of flesh, usually happening to exposed flesh and usually beginning on the surface or on the extremities. Hypothermia is a state where the body has lost heat and is at risk for continuing to lose more heat than it can produce, and commonly refers to the critical loss of heat in the body's core. All these conditions can vary from mild to severe, with the very real risk of death or disabling injury present at the severe end of the spectrum. Experiencing either frostbite or hypothermia in a blizzard situation is a dire challenge, and I reiterate that prevention is the key—treating either hypothermia or frostbite in the field during a blizzard is very difficult.

Preventive measures include wearing proper clothing, seeking or creating shelter from the storm, and eating and drinking adequately to keep your body's inner furnace burning. As a general rule, you should eat and drink more than you think you need when you are out in a wintry environment. On a somewhat peculiar note, there is some evidence that ibuprofen helps to prevent frostbite. Alcohol should be completely avoided when there is any possibility of developing cold-related problems.

It's also important to recognize the signs of developing hypothermia and frostbite, and to recognize the fact that the two conditions are often interrelated. Early or mild stages of frostbite are often called frostnip, and symptoms begin with painfully cold sensations in the afflicted area. Numbness and tingling are also common, as is an itchiness at the site. Sensation at the site will progress to more pronounced numbness, and the afflicted area will turn pale. There may be a period of alternating sensations of sharp

Windchill Chart

When the wind speed (mph) is								
Calm	5	10	15	20	25	30	35	40
At this temperature it will feel like (in degrees Fahrenheit):								
40	37	28	22	18	16	13	11	10
30	27	16	9	4	0	-2	-4	-6
20	16	4	-5	-10	-15	-18	-20	-21
10	6	-9	-18	-25	-29	-33	-35	-37
-5	-15	-21	-32	-39	-44	-48	-51	-53
-10	-21	-33	-45	-53	-59	-63	-67	-69
-20	-26	-46	-58	-67	-74	-79	-82	-85
-30	-36	-58	-72	-82	-88	-94	-98	-101
-40	-47	-70	-85	-96	-104	-109	-113	-116

TABLE COMPILED BY MARIAH HENRY, 2016

pain and numbness at the site, as the body alternately constricts blood vessels at the site to conserve blood and heat in favor of the body's core, and then dilates those vessels to keep the affected site from freezing.

If the situation causing the freezing flesh is not rectified, either by getting the victim to shelter or employing supplemental clothing or heat (as from a fire or chemical heat packs), further progression will lead to a state of uninterrupted numbness at the site. Still further progression will lead to the site becoming hard frozen, at which point the victim is at risk for permanent damage in the afflicted area. In more progressed stages, the afflicted area turns from pale to dark blue or black, as the oxygen-deprived and frozen tissues begin to die.

Failure to address the elements causing the frostbite can also lead to hypothermia. In the beginning, hypothermia presents as normal shivering and goose bumps, as well as some loss of dexterity in the hands and fingers—in short, the person is just plain cold. As things progress, however, the shivering becomes more pronounced, manual dexterity becomes ever more impaired, and muscles generally begin to stiffen as the person becomes more and more clumsy. At this point an afflicted individual can even behave a little like a drunk person, in that he or she might begin to stagger or stumble and have trouble walking in a straight line.

As things worsen, shivering becomes ever more violent and the affected person develops more and more trouble thinking and talking. Memory loss is noticeable, and the use of hands and fingers is nearly or even completely lost. Muscle rigidity sets in, as do confusion and sometimes

Warming up by a backcountry fire in the forest while on a back-country ski trip in Madison Mountain Range, southern Montana.
JERRY BREKKE

irrational behavior. The person may exhibit a state of withdrawal from surroundings and companions. A huge warning sign is when shivering stops and the person loses much or all consciousness. At that point hypothermia is an imminently life-threatening situation.

I went on a search and rescue for a lost snowshoer in the Old Faithful area of Yellowstone Park in March 1986. I was working as a park ranger at the time, and the snowshoer was reported as overdue from his outing in the late afternoon, so we did not initiate our search until after dark. The weather conditions were terrible, with a heavy and steady rain falling at a temperature just above the freezing point—a perfect recipe for hypothermia. When we finally caught up with the wayward snowshoer, he was far out on the Madison Plateau, many miles west of Old Faithful.

He was poorly clothed for conditions and in a seriously hypothermic state, to the point where he was exhausted, confused, and at times suicidal—he kept asking us to leave him alone so he could die in peace, and he had trouble remembering his own birthday or even his name. I remember having to shout at him repeatedly to startle him out of his torpor, over and over asking him simple questions like his home address and his birth date and name. To evacuate him back to Old Faithful, I finally had to extend the basket end of my ski pole to him, which he tucked under his armpit; he then held on to the shank of the pole with both hands while I snowshoed ahead and towed him along. I can't remember exactly what his temperature was when we finally got him back to Old Faithful, but I do remember that it was life-threateningly low. The wandering snowshoer from Brooklyn, New York, did make a full recovery, however.

Treating Hypothermia and Frostbite

Simply stated, a hypothermia victim must be rewarmed to the point where normal body temperature, especially core temperature, is restored. You need to get the victim out of the elements that caused the condition in the first place, first of all by moving the person to shelter. The shelter can be a heated building, if one is close enough at hand, or an emergency shelter like a lean-to or a wickiup set up in the backcountry. As discussed earlier, it's also important to take advantage of naturally sheltered spots, whether they're sheltered by vegetation or terrain. Building a fire, if possible, is a great solution—more than any other measure a cheery fire is likely to save the day both physically and psychologically. Changing the victim out of any wet clothes and replacing them with a dry outfit is a must. Placing bottles of warm water close to the person's body is another good solution, as are chemical heat packs.

Swaddling the person in blankets or a sleeping bag is another worthwhile measure; in severe cases, place the afflicted person in a sleeping bag along with someone else.

Of course, the second person should preferably be someone enjoying normal body temperature and metabolic function. Potential problems with this response include finding a sleeping bag large enough to accommodate two bodies, and the risk of chilling the second person to the point where you have doubled your hypothermia challenge. Also, if you try to evacuate the hypothermic person with a second person wrapped in the same package, you have doubled the amount of weight you have to tow or tote.

Do not warm up a hypothermic person too rapidly, and especially do not warm up the extremities first, as doing so may lead to heart problems for the victim. Severe, near death cases of hypothermia should be evaluated by medical professionals, even if you have successfully warmed up the person by the time you get to a hospital and the person seems to be OK.

Another cautionary note about dealing with frostbite: It's usually best to not try to thaw frozen flesh in the field. Even if the victim has frozen feet, it's still possible for that person to walk some distance. If you thaw frozen flesh in the field, it's likely that your victim will become a stretcher or tow sled case. If frozen flesh does thaw in the field, it is extremely important that you do not allow it to refreeze.

FIRST AID IN SNOW COUNTRY

For the purposes of this book, I must assume that the reader knows at least basic first aid, including CPR. This chapter deals mainly with how to administer first aid in a cold and snowy environment.

It's really quite simple in a basic sense: You have the same concerns as usual in terms of first aid—considerations like making sure an accident victim has a clear airway, is breathing, has a pulse, and so on. You also have to know how to stabilize broken bones and stop life-threatening bleeding—the difference is you have to know how to do all those things in a wintry setting while keeping the victim warm and dry.

In any snowy first-aid situation, it's important to keep the injured person out of the snow. Depending on circumstances, you might want to set up an aid station by clearing snow and perhaps building a shelter and/or a fire. In all circumstances you should place the injured party on some sort of tarp or pad to insulate the victim from the snow while you address the injury. Lying in the snow means getting wet and cold, and preventing that must always be foremost in your mind.

For first-aid supplies in winter, I recommend a large stock of 4×4 bandages, a space blanket(s), moleskin, ace wraps, mineral salt replacement tablets, lip balm (with a solar protection element), sunscreen, and a generous stock of gauze. These materials are in addition to all the survival and other winter gear recommended elsewhere in this book, such as parachute cord. In addition to many other repair and emergency uses, cord can be used in a lot of first-aid applications as well, such as binding splints to a broken limb, or binding extra clothing items to the same broken limb to keep it warm in cold temperatures.

TREATING INJURIES FROM SKIING OR SNOWSHOEING

Because of the nature of snowshoeing and skiing, falling is common. Falls lead to sprains, strains, and fractures due to the wrenching mechanisms of injury. Setting broken bones and stabilizing sprains and strains are the same in snowy environments as in any other season of the year, with the primary difference being that you have to take extra care in swaddling and otherwise protecting the injured site from the cold. Close monitoring for developing cold-related problems must continue at frequent intervals after injuries have been stabilized. Chemical heat packs or warm water bottles are again a good idea, as long as they are not placed directly against the injured person's skin. The injured site should be kept dry, which means keeping it (and the entire body of the injured person) out of the snow.

Collisions with trees are also a common occurrence with skiers. They can also lead to broken bones, of course, and can also cause facial injuries. As with wrenching falls, leg injuries can occur in collisions with trees and other objects, but collisions are more likely to cause injuries to the upper body. Generally, injuries to the arms and shoulders are not as difficult to deal with as leg injuries, because in most cases the victim can still stand upright and hopefully will be able to walk or snowshoe. Poling while skiing is obviously a problem with an injured shoulder or arm, however.

There are commercially produced rescue sleds made for evacuating injured people from the snowy backcountry. Since it's highly improbable that you will have one along when a backcountry injury occurs, it's good to know that an emergency evacuation sled can be fashioned by cross-country skiers by using the blade from an avalanche

In addition to splinting and stabilization, injured extremities require extra padding and swaddling in cold weather. PETER LEWIS/ SOLO SCHOOL, CONWAY, NEW HAMPSHIRE

shovel and the skis of the injured person. First, remove the handle of the shovel from the blade (most avalanche shovels are constructed for easy disassembly). Next, tie the tips of the skis to the cupped side of the shovel blade, then tie the spread-out tails of the skis to the ends of the shovel handle. That way the assembly takes on the profile of a V, with the skis at the same angle as they would be if a person skiing downhill had them in the snowplowing position. For additional cross members to span the space between the V-shaped skis, you can use ski poles or sticks. The injured party is then placed on top of the creation to be towed to safety by one or more rescuers.

Cargo sleds are designed for pulling your gear along while you trek on cross-country skis or snowshoes. If you happen to have one of these in your group, and it's large enough, you might be able to employ it to evacuate an injured comrade.

Also, depending on circumstances, you can build a litter out of poles and sticks bound together with parachute cord or some other strong but lightweight cord. You should not try this unless you're certain you can do an adequate job of stringing the litter together. And you should not try to carry a person out on any sort of litter if you do not have sufficient personnel on hand to do the job—dumping an injured person off a litter while in transit might worsen the injury.

Litter transport in a first-aid evacuation from the backcountry is probably best considered when the snow is not too deep for walking, or when snowshoes are available for those carrying the litter. In most circumstances, rescuers on skis are not able to do a very good job of carrying a litter.

Great care must be taken when carrying an injured party on an evacuation litter. PETER LEWIS/SOLO SCHOOL, CONWAY, NEW HAMPSHIRE

If you and your group are on cross-country skis, however, there is a way to make the skis nonslip, so that you can more or less walk on them as though they were simply long, skinny snowshoes.

You can arrest the gliding properties of skis by wrapping them in parachute cord or something similar. Begin by tying some sort of one-way slipknot around the ski just a couple of inches behind its tip, then loop a series of half hitches around the ski at intervals of 6 inches or so. Continue wrapping half hitches around the ski as you work back toward the binding, at which point pull the whole chain of hitches as tight as you can and tie the cord off to the back side of the binding with a simple clove hitch. Return the cord to the front of the binding and tie it securely. Then extend the cord back to the rear of the binding and begin a new series of half hitches as you weave a chain toward the back of the ski. On the last wrap near the tail of the ski, tie the whole thing off with a clove hitch. You should wind up with somewhere around fifteen or sixteen wraps along the entire length of the ski. The parachute cord in effect forms cross-stitches across the bottom of the ski, which prevent the ski from sliding forward or backward, and the segments of cord extending lengthways along the ski between half hitches keep the ski from sliding sideways, as it might on a sidehill.

INJURIES FROM SNOWMOBILING

Snowmobiles are big, powerful, and fast machines, so many snowmobile accidents result in truly serious injuries. I have seen feet and lower legs badly mangled after they became entangled in a machine's track. In my home area, and everywhere that snowmobiles are used, for that matter, it's quite common for snowmobilers to die when they collide with trees or other obstacles. Snowmobiles also collide with each other, of course, often resulting in serious injuries or death to their operators and passengers. Snow machines are prone to rolling over or flipping end for end, and because they are so heavy—some models weigh more than 800 pounds—they can do major damage to an operator or passenger if they wind up on top of the person in a tumble. Just a few years ago, a woman was killed in an accident near where I live when the snowmobile she was driving flipped and landed on top of her.

Snowmobiles offer an advantage over skis and snowshoes, in that if the machine involved in a mishap is still operable, or if there are other snow machines nearby, they can be used to more quickly evacuate an injured person. If a snowmobile tow sled is available, it can quite readily be made into a litterlike sled for use in hauling an injured person. Most snowmobile seats are large enough that, depending on the nature of the injury involved, the injured person can ride on the back of the machine while a second person drives, provided the driver

If available, a snowmobile tow sled may be used for evacuations.

is skilled and careful. Of course, depending on the nature of the injury, the injured person might be able to operate a snowmobile independently to reach assistance.

If a tow sled is used for evacuation, it's a good idea to place a tarp, or better yet some sort of pad, on the bottom of the sled for the injured person to sit on. If the sled is large enough, and some of them are, a second person could ride in the sled to assist the injured party. Again, great care should be taken by the driver of the machine pulling the sled, as riding in a sled can be bouncy and rough at the best of times, and they are prone to tipping over on sidehills.

Snowmobiles have the further capacity to make a quick run for help, if there are enough people and machines on hand to spare someone for such a run. Only the people involved can make such a decision as to how best to employ the personnel and other resources at hand.

Hypothermia and frostbite are ever-present concerns in the snowy backcountry, and those concerns are greatly amplified after an injury has occurred. Two other concerns of importance are sunburn and snowblindness.

SUNBURN AND SNOWBLINDNESS

It might seem a little counterintuitive to worry about sunburn in the winter in the high latitudes where snow lingers for long periods of time and where most winter recreationists pursue their enthusiasms. But sun reflecting off snow can be a powerful force. The obvious solution to this problem is to carry and apply sunscreen. Failure to do so will almost always result in sunburn, especially in late winter when the sun has climbed higher into the sky and has gained more power than in midwinter. Sunburn can be more than just an irritation and a factor for developing skin cancer in the long run. In the short term it can sap energy that is better saved for recreation or work or some sort of emergency.

Snowblindness is a potentially serious condition resulting from exposure to the brightness of the sun shining from the sky coupled with its reflection off snow. It is also called photokeratitis, which in essence is simply sunburned eyeballs, and can result from any bright light, such as an arc welder, the light in a tanning booth, or exposure to sunny conditions on the water or on a sandy beach. But the risk of blindness from bright light is greatest during sunny weather on snow, especially at high elevations. Unbroken snowfields reflect far more light than do either water or sand, and levels of harmful radiation from the sun are greatly increased as you travel upward to higher elevations.

I suffered a case of snowblindness once, in March 1997. Early that month I traveled to a remote area in Wyoming to clear the snow from four buildings used to lodge summer tourists. I lost my sunglasses somewhere along the way, and the area was so remote that it would have taken me a full day of travel to go somewhere to replace them. At that point in my life I was so macho I thought I could get along without them, so I did not take the time to procure another pair of sunglasses, or to fashion some sort of substitute from materials in the area.

After a few days of working on the roofs in the brightness of the late winter sun, I came down with a classic case of snowblindness. My eyes were red and watery, and also itchy, as though I had gotten sand in them. As time went on, my vision darkened, to the point where everything I looked at had the appearance of an underexposed photograph. Fortunately, I finished my first hitch of work in the area and returned home for a few days, where I got out of the sun and my vision recovered. I made certain I had a new pair of sunglasses by the time I returned to my next stint of roof clearing work.

As the above anecdote illustrates, prevention of snowblindness is usually a pretty simple matter—just wear eye protection. Either good quality sunglasses or goggles will work, as long as you make sure you have them along and wear them whenever you are out on bright snowscapes. On extended trips in the backcountry, it's probably a good idea to take along a spare set of glasses or, if you are traveling in a group, to take along at least a couple pairs of replacements to be shared among the group if someone loses or breaks theirs.

If you somehow lose your eyewear in a remote area, as I did in 1997, it is possible to fabricate a replacement. Arctic peoples used to make goggles with small slits that allowed for vision but prevented the passage of enough bright light to burn the eyes. They used naturally occurring materials like antler, ivory, bone, driftwood, and tree bark and tied their carved goggles in place with sinew or other cord they also had concocted from materials they found in nature. You can do something similar—if you don't happen to have any caribou antler or walrus ivory on hand, you can carve a piece of wood or tree bark into a Lone Ranger–style mask with narrow eye slits. And if you don't happen to have any polar bear sinew along on your backcountry trip, you can use a piece of the all-purpose parachute cord to do the job. If you do carve a mask, make sure you also carve an inset to allow for the bridge of your nose.

Another, probably faster and easier, way to fashion emergency snow goggles is to use some of the duct tape that I recommend carrying—more is better than less—in a wrap around your ski pole, or wherever and however you find it convenient to carry. Take two strips of tape about 10 or 12 inches long and paste them together, sticky side to sticky side. Next, cut narrow eye slits in the face of the mask, then punch small holes into the two opposite ends of the strip of tape and inset a short piece of parachute cord through the holes before tying the whole creation around the back of your head.

Another trick to help reduce the glare reflecting into the eyes is to smudge a little charcoal or mud high on your cheeks, just below the level of each eye. Yet another idea is to wear a tight-fitting balaclava with narrow eye slits, although wearing such a garment might well result in overheating if you are actively moving about in conditions other than very cold weather.

If you are careless, or macho as I was in that 1997 incident, and come down with a case of snowblindness, the RX for the condition is to first get out of the bright sun and snow. You can further ease the inflammation by staying in an interior room or somewhere else with reduced light, or by using a dark mask over the eyes. A moistened cloth will help reduce the sandy, itchy feeling.

Snowblindness can be a serious condition—literal blindness can be a temporary or even permanent result. Even if the condition is temporary, it obviously can have serious ramifications for anyone afflicted in the backcountry. As with almost every other problem discussed in this book, preventing the condition by using proper eyewear is worth so much more than any response after the fact.

SNOW CAMPING

Snow camping can be done for fun, as a way to enjoy an extended experience in the outdoors during the winter season; or it can be done as a survival measure, as a way of taking refuge from the elements after some sort of mishap has stranded you in the wintry outdoors. Either way, your level of skill and ability will determine whether you camp in comfort, or whether you camp in misery and perhaps threaten your own survival.

TENT CAMPING IN THE SNOW

It is possible to camp in a tent in snow country, especially if the snow isn't all that deep. Tents, of course, range in size from small backpacker units just large enough to accommodate one person to canvas wall tents as large as cabins. Because most of us aren't strong enough to carry such a large and heavy tent on our backs, the latter are usable only for roadside camping, or on a horse trip that includes enough stock to pack in the heavy tent and all of its accessories.

I have camped in such a tent with luxuries like cots and woodstoves many times. Again, one problem with such an outfit is that it usually is feasible only in the early part of the winter, or until the snow gets too deep. If you are caught in the backcountry when the truly heavy and lasting

A well set up tent camp in snow country. LISA CULPEPPER/CULPEPPER PHOTOGRAPHY

snows fall in late autumn or early winter, then you and your outfit might be marooned in conditions where your vehicle and/or your horses are overwhelmed by the snow.

In a more classic winter scenario, such as a cross-country ski or snowshoe trip into the backcountry, a smaller tent can be employed. There is always the tradeoff, of course, between the considerations of weight and substance. A single-walled, lightweight tent is easier to carry, but it is not as warm as a double-walled tent and is much more prone to condensation than a double-walled unit. Frosted condensation from the exhalations of sleeping campers is a substantial problem while camping in a tent in cold weather.

FABRICATED SHELTERS

A shelter can also be constructed out of natural materials in the backcountry, building a structure such as a wickiup or a lean-to (see the Hiking in Snow Country chapter). They are feasible, for the most part, only where the snow is not all that deep, and obviously you can build them only where there are suitable building materials available—that is, somewhere that is wooded.

Another factor to consider is that in this world of 7.5 billion people, our protected natural areas are comparatively few and small, and using naturally occurring materials to build structures such as wickiups and lean-tos is today usually considered too consumptive. It's considered not acceptable to build such shelters unless the situation is dire, such as a case where your snowmobile has broken down in remote country, or a member of your party has been injured and you have to hunker down while someone goes for help or while you make the preparations necessary for an evacuation.

SNOW SHELTERS

Various types of snow shelters can be constructed where the snow is deep and the weather consistently below freezing. Snow shelters including igloos, snow caves, quinzhees, and snow trenches can be constructed on a simple recreational outing, or they can be built in an emergency to survive a life-threatening situation that has developed in the wake of an unexpected turn of events in the backcountry.

Igloo Construction

Almost everyone is familiar with the basic outline of the igloo. The domed architecture of an igloo provides for a strong structure—in the Arctic there are stories of igloos supporting the weight of polar bears that have climbed onto their roofs—and its strength increases as the snow in the walls and roof sets up still further after construction is

Polar bear researcher Chuck Jonkel shows a group of students how to build an igloo on the shore of Hudson Bay, near Churchill, Manitoba.

complete. There are tricks to building one, however, with the first necessity being a small snow saw. A bona fide snow saw usually comes with a sheath so that it's not only easier to carry but also so the blade is not exposed in your pack to cut things you don't want to have cut.

Site selection is one of the first considerations when deciding to build an igloo or any other snow structure. The site should be flat, or nearly so, and it should be completely out of the way of any possible avalanche danger. Next you have to find snow that is amenable to cutting blocks—ideally a bank of drifted or otherwise well consolidated snow that is firm enough to hold in block form after you saw it out. If the snow is too densely set up, however, it will lack the tiny air pockets necessary to give your igloo its desired insulative value.

If you can't find a source of snow that is suitably set up for cutting blocks, you can use a shovel to mix snow from different layers on the ground into a heap, and then leave it alone for a few hours while the snow hardens. This requires time and patience, of course, and is not ideal if your emergency calls for a quick response. If you do resort to piling up snow in preparation for cutting igloo blocks, be sure to thoroughly mix snow from different layers within the snowpack in order to get the consolidated mix you need to form firm blocks.

OK, say you have either found or concocted a bank of suitable snow from which to cut the snow blocks for your igloo. It works most efficiently to cut the blocks out of the snowbank in a geometric pattern, similar to the pattern of excavations in a stone quarry. Block size depends somewhat on your own judgment, but each one should be roughly the size of a shoe box. It often works best to have just one person saw the blocks. When two or more people cut blocks for the same igloo, it seems that each person involved has his or her own sense of size and proportion, and often the blocks of varying size don't mesh well.

You also need to pack down the snow at the site where you intend to build your igloo, which preferably will be a site that is slightly elevated, so that the floor of your igloo will be higher than the level of the surface of the surrounding snowfield. That's so the living space of your finished structure will be a little elevated, the better to hold warmth inside the igloo. If you can't find a spot that is slightly elevated, you can heap up a little snow with your shovel to make a higher floor. Either way, it works well to tamp the site down with skis or snowshoes so the floor will be firm when you move into your shelter.

Begin by laying your cut blocks in a circle to outline the base of your igloo. Subsequent layers of blocks will need to spiral upward as they are laid, and also progressively lean more and more toward the inside of the structure so that ultimately it will close off at the apex of its dome. You can accomplish this either by quarrying blocks cut on the correct angles, or by first laying square blocks and then cutting the necessary angles after the blocks have been set in place. Give each block a gentle tap as it is laid in place to seat it firmly to the blocks on which it is resting, but don't tap the block too hard because it might break. Ideally the length of each block will span the seam of two blocks in the next layer below—just as bricks in a wall are laid so that each one overlays a seam between two lower bricks.

Continue spiraling upward until the final keystone block is set in place to seal off the top of the dome. It works really well to have at least two people involved: one to cut and carry blocks to the construction site and then pass them over the wall to the block layer working inside the growing igloo. The final block might have to be passed through the door of the igloo and then lifted up through the last hole in the dome at an angle, after which it can be turned and fitted into place by gravity as the builder gets his or her hands out of the way at the last moment.

It works best to saw the door out of the finished wall after the basic layout of the igloo has been established and the walls have risen to a level at least a couple feet higher than the crown of the door. After the door has been cut out, an entryway can be added in the form of a short tunnel. This configuration helps keep wind out of the inside of your igloo and, if you have built an elevated floor, any heat inside the igloo will tend to rise into the domed interior rather than waft out the door.

Shovels full of snow can be flung onto the finished structure, and the powdered snow gently rubbed with a gloved or mittened hand to chink any spaces left between blocks. You can light a candle, lantern, or camp stove inside your igloo to not only provide heat and light, but also glaze the inside surface of your structure, which provides an extra margin of structural strength as well as another seal against wind. A glazed surface is also less likely to collect vapor or meltwater on snowy protuberances, from which it might drip onto occupants. If your igloo is large enough, you

Biologist Chuck Jonkel shows a group the finer points of igloo construction at Old Faithful, Yellowstone National Park

can also build benches inside the structure that you can use for tables, seats, or sleeping surfaces. As always when camping in the snow, it's very important to keep yourself dry while building an igloo—the snow is good insulation against the frigid outdoors, but you have to keep yourself insulated from the snow.

It's amazing how much warmer it is inside an igloo than it is outside, especially in very cold weather, and especially in windy conditions. Experiments have shown that there can be as much as a 70°F temperature difference (or even more) between the air inside an igloo compared to the air outside. Several times I have had the chance to spend some time inside igloos on the shores of Hudson Bay, on trips I took to the area to photograph polar bears. The weather I experienced on those trips was some of the harshest I have ever seen. The temperatures themselves weren't all that extreme—usually in the range of 5°F to −5°F—but the winds blowing off the bay were ferocious and saturated with humidity.

Inside the igloos the winds were blocked, of course, and the temperature of the inside air warmed noticeably immediately upon enclosure, even before we lighted a candle or any other source of heat.

Snow Caves and Quinzhees

There are other snow shelters you can construct for either recreational or emergency reasons. A snow cave is dug into an existing snowbank, with a narrow entryway and an enlarged living space in its interior. Snow of a certain consolidation must be selected for this type of shelter—if the snow is not sufficiently set up, your snow cave may collapse on you. If you can find and identify suitable snow, a cave has an advantage over an igloo in that it can be quicker and easier to build. As with an igloo, you want your entryway to be lower than your living space, again because warm air rises, and you want whatever heat you generate to stay with you and not dissipate to the outside. You can also build shelves for sleeping and table use inside a snow cave similar to those inside an igloo.

Lisa Culpepper appears pleased with her digs, in a snow cave, Washburn Mountain Range, Yellowstone National Park. LISA CULPEPPER/CULPEPPER PHOTOGRAPHY

A quinzhee is a snow cave that you dig out of snow you have heaped up yourself, something you might choose to do in an area where you can't find a suitable drift or other natural deposit of consolidated snow.

A quinzhee takes some time—probably close to half a day—to construct. First, you have to find a site with enough snow to do the job, as well as a site that meets all other necessary concerns, such as safety from avalanche, wind protection, and so forth. Next, you have to spend the time to shovel enough snow into a pile to result in a final structure of suitable size. Then, and most important, you have to wait several hours after heaping for the snow to set up sufficiently before you begin to hollow out the pile. Failure to wait long enough may result in your quinzhee collapsing while excavation is in progress. In the end your quinzhee will probably look a lot like an igloo, only you will have built it by hollowing out a mound of snow rather than building the dome out of many sawn blocks.

With any of these domed structures, it's a good idea to poke a small hole near the top of the dome, possibly by using the tip of a ski pole, to allow for air circulation. This is especially important if you are using any accessory that burns oxygen and exhausts carbon monoxide and carbon dioxide, such as a lantern, a camp stove, or even a simple candle. Also, with the construction of any snow shelter, you probably will get wet while building it, so you should plan ahead to have some way to dry out, or at least plan to change into dry clothes after the work is done. And because it takes quite a time investment to build a snow shelter, they are preferable when you plan to stay in the same place for more than just one night—unless, of course, you are building the shelter in response to an emergency situation and urgently need the shelter for survival.

Snow Trenches

The snow shelter that is probably the simplest and fastest to build is a snow trench. It is, as the name implies, simply a trench that you dig into the snow that is long enough and wide enough to accommodate you and any gear you want to take with you into the shelter. You construct a roof over your trench by first laying skis, ski poles, tree limbs, or anything else you have on hand to bridge the gap over the surface of the trench. After the skis, poles, or other items have been placed over the trench, you cover them with a tarp and then weigh down the tarp with snow. The snow on top of the tarp not only holds it in place, but it also affords a bit of insulation to the person sleeping or sheltering in the trench. You can leave a slight opening in your tarp some-where along its span to allow for air circulation.

A drawback with the trench shelter is that the ceiling is not strong. If new snow of any consequence is falling, you may have to get up in the night to shovel some of it away, or else run the risk of your roof collapsing on top of you. Another drawback is that the relatively thin roof does not provide as much insulation as the thicker roof of a quinzhee, igloo, or snow cave, although the lateral walls of a trench, formed by the continuous snowpack around you, have almost unlimited insulative value.

ESSENTIAL WINTER EQUIPMENT

Following is a list of essential winter equipment that you should have with you in a winter camping or survival situation, no matter what sort of shelter you use.

- ❑ A down vest or jacket

- ❑ Two one-quart water bottles

- ❑ Extra food

- ❑ Knife

- ❑ Flashlight or headlamp and extra batteries
- ❑ Camp stove with one pint of fuel per person per day
- ❑ Toilet paper
- ❑ Waterproof matches and cigarette lighter
- ❑ Candle(s)
- ❑ Warm-up pants
- ❑ Shell garments
- ❑ Spare gloves or mittens
- ❑ Spare hat
- ❑ Ground cloths/tarp
- ❑ Space blanket(s)
- ❑ Sunscreen
- ❑ Lip balm (with sunscreen)
- ❑ Compass and maps of the area you're traveling
- ❑ Notebook and pencil (pens don't work well in the cold)
- ❑ Down socks or booties
- ❑ First-aid kit
- ❑ Sitting/sleeping pad

As you can see, a lot of the items on this list are for staying warm as well as insulated and dry from the snow. That's an overriding concern—you have to stay dry, which means you can't allow yourself to get wet from melting snow. And if you get wet from perspiration during exertion, you have to figure out a way to dry yourself, whether by warming by a fire, changing clothes, or some other means. During a winter trip it's a good idea to take advantage of any clear, sunny weather to warm and dry yourself and your equipment, even if you have to delay your travel schedule to do so. It's amazing how much warmth the low-angle, midwinter sun can afford when its rays bounce off the snow and winds are calm. And even in very snowy environments, it's often possible to find sites that are completely or nearly snow-free. Tree wells or wind-scoured sites on south-facing slopes are likely places to find such spots.

In summary, on any winter trip you must continually be mindful of a few basic concerns: staying dry, warm, well fed, and well hydrated. You also need to keep these in mind for all of your companions—you have to watch out for each other. These concerns should be taken into account in everything you do, including the little things. One example is to heat water on your camp stove before bedtime to pour into water bottles to place near your body while you sleep—they really help keep you warm at night. You should also have liquid water close at hand for drinking through the night and in the morning when you wake up. Another tip about water bottles on a winter trip, whether in your sleeping bag with you at night or in your backpack while